What's a Nice Person Like Me

Doing in a Body Like This?

Dr. Neecie Moore

Validation press

Published by Validation Press

Copyright © 2002 by Dr. Neecie Moore
Cover by Scott Hamilton
Book design and composition by Chris Roth
Images copyright www.arttoday.com. and Zedcor Desk Gallery

Printed in the United States of America
ISBN: 0-9660700-3-8

Other books by Dr. Neecie Moore:
The Missing Link:
    The Facts about Glyconutrients
Designing Your Life with Designer Foods:
    The Facts about Phytochemicals
The Miracle in Aloe Vera:
    The Facts about Polymannans
Bountiful Health Boundless Energy Brilliant Youth:
    The Facts about DHEA
A Long and Healthy Life:
    The Facts about High Level Wellness

First Edition
1 2 3 4 5 6 7 8 9 10

$17.95 Softcover

Contents

*Consult your physician
before making any major changes in
your dietary or exercise programs.*

Dedication

In loving memory of:

Dora Belle Parks

As my neighbor when I was growing up, Dora was like an auntie or young grandmother to me. She always had a moment to ask about my day, to laugh about a story I might tell her, or to teach me something about gardening. She brought much joy and comfort to us as we started our new lives in La Porte, Texas. Today, I am certain that she is tending the most gorgeous, well-manicured garden in heaven!

Ima Harris

I promised Ima that I would acknowledge her in my book, but never planned to do so in memory of her. She won a long, courageous battle with cancer this past year and is now singing with the angels in heaven. Oh how we miss her!

I dedicate this book to Freida Kawar, my dear friend. I met Freida as the owner of Young At Heart, an adult day care for seniors with memory challenges.

We placed my dad, who has Alzheimer's, with Freida several years ago. She took excellent care of him until we had to place him in full-time care.

Freida, along with her excellent staff (Joyce, Barbara, Leah, Carol, and many others) not only cared for my dad, but cared for our whole family.

During some of the toughest days of our family history, when we were losing my dad (Alzheimer's is a disease where you lose your loved one twice...once to Alzheimer's and then to death), Freida was there to support us, love us, and pray for us.

I've never seen anyone with the love, compassion, and devotion to Alzheimer's patients that she has. She has inspired me tremendously.

My prayer is that I may be half the person Freida is when I grow up!

I love you, Freida! God bless you richly!

SPECIAL THANKS

To Caroline MacNeill and Luke, for believing in my project, and in me, and being such great cheerleaders.

To Wil and Wilma Watson, for being a constant source of inspiration and modeling true love and devotion.

To Pat Heath, Ed Learned, Traci Lopez, Cheri Henderson, Julia Phelps, and all of the other caregivers at ActivCare Glen Eagles who have found joy in my dad, Red, and have honored him with their love and kindness.

To Pastor Lee and Sharon Lebsack, for giving me a place to feel at home and for giving excellent spiritual direction.

To Pastor Gary and Tammy Macdonald, for loving me, supporting me, and praying with me through the valley, and for rejoicing with me on the mountaintop!

To Pastor Jeff and Barbie Ogg, for being the greatest big brother and little sis I could ever hope for. Thanks, too, for singing to me while I was in the valley and lifting my spirits to the mountaintop!

To Michael Gorton, Dr. Byron Brooks, Gina Fidnick, Christopher Phelan, and Julius Minja for an incredible trip up Mt. Kilimanjaro. My life will never be the same!

To all of the wonderful people who have been such an important part of making my dream come true at Let's Celebrate!, Inc.: Mary Klaasen (my dear friend and mentor), Tami Bullard, Lowell and Shirley Thomas, Kevin Young ("Cousin K"), Clay Arnold, Nancy Cunningham, Ben Watson,

Saunde O'kelley, Bradley Kendall, Terry and Susan (my sis "Susie") Rock, and last, but not least, my partner, Gary Watson.

Ruana Grace, my sister. For always being there for me, always believing in me, and for being my very best friend.

To my angel mother, Sissie, and my precious dad, Red, who taught me to go for my dreams and never give up. They have been my greatest cheerleaders of all!

ACKNOWLEDGEMENTS

I would like to acknowledge:

My daughters, Andrea, Kelli, Colleen and Twyla, for being so patient with my absence while I developed my dream.

My wonderful fristers, Mary Ellen, Anita, Shari, Susan, and Ginny, without whom I could have never developed my dream and stayed persistent through the storms.

My Alzheimer's Support Group, and especially Debbie Rhinehart, who have provided support through the joys and the tears. To Lyle Saunders, my friend and running buddy, for being a loyal supporter of my project.

My dear friends, Vivienne Mccurley (Sug), Helen Cox, and Shirley Duncan, for taking us in as family and giving my family a place to get connected.

My retreat friends, Kathy Thompson, Allene Bradt, Kelley Mackay, Linda Dugger, and Janel Reid for letting me join them in having a great time and to my dear friend, Bonnie Floyd for touching us all so deeply!

My church singing team, Cheryl, Marty, Hilary, Al, and Marion, our awesome leader, Amber Rhoads, and to the band: RO, JP, Kevin, Michael, and Tim. You all inspire me to be a better person for God! And to Dave Stephens, for having enough faith in me to let me join the team as a brand new member. (I miss you!)

The Ladies Ministree Board— Frieda, Shirley, Vivienne, Sharon, Mary Lou, Julie, and Joni, who have been so faithful in their love and support.

Gina Anderson, for getting my dad to sing "In the Garden" with her at a moment when we thought we were losing him!

My talented and gifted friend (and joy), Craig Thompson for sharing dreams with me and encouraging me to journalize in the midst of the storm!

My patriotic red, white, and blue friends, Judy Harris and Ellen Morgan, for always taking time for our little expeditions.

Dr. Sterling Sightler (her dear mother, Betty Sightler, and her fun husband Dr. Marty Jones), for keeping my mother healthy and making her a 10-year survivor of cancer.

Jerry Kelly, for providing moments of sanity and excellent guidance with humor and compassion.

Sharon and Charles Burton and all of the Overcomers, for being lights of hope, faithful friends, and examples of God's grace and mercy.

Debbi Morel, for being my sister through thick and thin.

What's a Nice Person Like Me...

All of my "family" at CLA, so excellently led by Lee and Sharon Lebsack, Jack and Mary Lou Dial, Billy and Sharon Abbe, Don and Marily Blair, Scott and Dana Olson, Vince and Tiffany Ford, Wayne and Jamie Geer, Dave and Cynthia Ericson, Gina and Paul Anderson, and Amber and Ronald Rhoads. I am truly blessed!

Beverly Rich, for showing up at just the right moment!

And especially to all of the wonderful folks who work with Validation Press, including designer Chris Roth, editor Sara Noland, and cover designer Scott Hamilton, for taking my project, believing in it, and for doing their magic.

Introduction

What you learn in this book will surprise you and may change your life!

Over the past 10 years, I have had the tremendous privilege of addressing audiences all over the world. Whether in Gothenburg, Sweden, or Dallas, Texas, the most frequently asked questions reflect the same theme: weight loss and energy levels.

I've seen the same despair in the eyes of women and men of every age, ethnic origin, socioeconomic group, and educational background.

Why can't I lose this weight?

Will I ever regain the energy I used to have?

What on earth can I do to change the way I look?

Will I ever feel like I have enough energy to make it through the day again?

Will I ever get back into the jeans hanging in the back of my closet?

I am always touched by what I see deep within the eyes of those asking me the questions. I see, hear, and feel the pain, the fear, the disgust, the despair. That is what moves me to reach out and attempt to make a difference. That's the reason for this book.

Several factors make these questions very difficult to answer. For example, changing caloric intake may not be what is needed; increasing exercise may or may not address the issue; and it's not easy to keep the weight off when you do lose it.

Sharing facts about weight loss and energy recovery is not enough. If it were, there wouldn't be countless Americans and others around the globe attempting to win what often feels like a losing battle. We are consumed with finding the answers to drooping energy and tipping scales.

I've spent the past 15 years devouring everything written about health, wellness, fitness, energy recovery, and weight loss. I've read articles in magazines, I've read books, I've read medical journals.

I'd love to promise you that as a result of my studies, the magical answers follow in the pages of this book. In all honesty, I must report that there are no magical answers; there aren't even any easy answers!

But I strongly encourage you to read on. What you learn in this book will surprise you and may change your life!

Several weeks ago, a colleague came to me and said, "I am at the worst point in my life. I've tried so many eating plans; I can't even remember what is nutritionally good for my body. I've combined so many of them I feel certain that I've destroyed my metabolism. I don't even care about my weight anymore. I just want to feel like I won't pass out from exhaustion before I finish my shower every morning. Is there any hope, or is this just the glory of life when approaching 50?"

We laughed together, but I detected the despair behind the laughter. I assured her that what she was describing was not simply the "glory of life when approaching 50!" Over the next 10 minutes, I summarized what you will find in the pages of this book. Her response: "I can do that...I can do that for life! So hurry up and finish the book!" I saw the flicker of hope. The hope I trust you will find as you read these pages.

But more than hope is required: You must have resolve, resolve to live a life beyond extraordinary...a life that is only available to those who are willing to make it happen!

Chapter 1

Encouragement

What is different about your program and why should I try it?

I've tried everything.

I know I'd feel better if I weighed less, but I just can't sustain my energy on a diet.

I just can't seem to change what I'm eating.

I know exercise is supposed to energize you, but I'm already below zero…so where do I find enough energy to get started?

I can't bear another starvation diet.

Those are just a few of the comments I've heard as I've listened to the struggles of men and women who have attempted to lose weight and keep it off. Similar questions come from people who have attempted to reclaim the energy they once experienced and yearn to regain.

Obviously these comments are NOT isolated! The subtitles of weight loss and energy books correlate to those cries:

Secrets of Radiant Health and Energy

Drop Pounds, Feel Great, and Never Go Hungry Again!

Invigorating Ways to Revitalize Your Life

A Short and Simple Way to Eat Naturally, Lose Weight, and Live a Healthier Life

The Art of Bringing New Energy Into Your Life

How to Lose Weight Step-By-Step Even After You've Failed at Dieting

You are probably asking yourself, and wanting to ask me before you read any further: What is different about your program and why should I try it?

GREAT QUESTION!

The truth is—I have no miraculous answers, I have no revolutionary new ideas, and I have no magical formulas. What I do have is a summary of the research on energy and weight loss, including a compilation of what I believe to be the healthiest, most life-changing plans. I know you are eager to read it, but there are a few things you must understand if you are to succeed.

An eating plan in and of itself is insufficient to get you the results you desire, the results you deserve. It is also necessary to examine the physiological, psychological, and spiritual factors that drive your eating, your exercise (or lack of), and your lifestyle. Don't simply read past this in your eagerness to learn more about the eating plan.

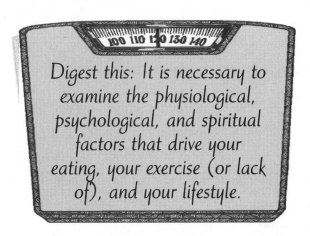

Digest this: It is necessary to examine the physiological, psychological, and spiritual factors that drive your eating, your exercise (or lack of), and your lifestyle.

As a matter of fact, find a pen. Research indicates that you are much more likely to remember something if you write it down. Fill in the statement below:

It is necessary to examine the

_____

_____

and

_____

factors that drive my eating, my

_____

(or lack of it), and my

_____

Now that you have written it, say it out loud. You must understand that 20 percent of your success depends on a good plan, but 80 percent depends on your psychology. Eighty percent of your success depends on what drives your eating, your exercise (or lack of), and your lifestyle.

Whether you have chosen to read this book because you have a mild interest in learning some tips, or whether you are in a desperate situation, I believe that YOU can achieve the health, fitness, vitality, and image you desire. Yes, YOU! I don't care how many diets you have tried, how many programs you've followed, how much weight you have lost and gained back. You can do this!

The story of the little train has inspired us with the words: "I think I can! I think I can! I think I can!" These words need to be bolstered with more resolve to: "I know I can! I know I can! I know I can!"

Chapter 2

Weight Loss in General

To effectively achieve the
weight loss you desire, and
maintain that new weight,
you must be willing to make
a change for life!

I f you have tried and failed at weight loss, you are not alone! Research has shown that 95 percent of people who have lost weight by restricting their caloric intake have regained it all within five years (Ikeda, 2000).

Surveys in 1992 indicated that 40 percent of adult women and 24 percent of men were trying to lose weight. In addition, 28 percent were attempting to maintain their weight (NIH, 1992). That means that in 1992, almost 70 percent of the adult population was concerned with their weight!

Odds are that you were one of them! And if you weren't among those concerned in 1992, chances are that you are now.

Actually, achieving weight loss has a fairly easy formula...stop eating! In my seminars, when I'm told "I've tried EVERYTHING!"...I always respond with this:

"Really? Have you fasted for 40 days and nights?" This response always leaves them speechless and off of dead center for a second or two. Getting you off of dead center of your defeating beliefs is part of what must be done to ensure your success.

No, this program is not about fasting! However, it is about eliminating your defeating beliefs about what is possible. The same defeating beliefs about weight loss also hinder your success at keeping the weight off when you reach your goal.

Popular magazine covers boast claims such as "Drop 10 pounds in six days!" My guess is that if you followed each of their formulas, you could achieve the promised results.

But what happens after you get to the goal? Perhaps they should tell the rest of the story: "Drop 10 pounds in six days...and gain them back in just three days!"

Let's do an honest self-assessment. How many times have you been through that routine? And, more importantly, how many more times do you care to repeat it? Hopefully…NONE!

To effectively achieve the weight loss you desire, and maintain that new weight, you must be willing to make a change for life! That's right— a change that will last longer than the five-day to six-week torture that you have subjected yourself to again and again.

I can hear you right now: "Neecie, do you mean I have no other alternative than to live through this torture for the rest of my life?"

Absolutely not! The key is in finding a lifestyle (of eating, of thinking, of exercising, of making choices) that is not torturous and that doesn't feel like deprivation.

Is there any such thing? Most people think not. Recently, a minister on staff at my church began shrinking. I noticed week by week that his face was thinning and his waistline was contracting. When asked by a congregation member how he did it, he replied with great disdain: "Well, it's easy. If it tastes good, spit it out!"

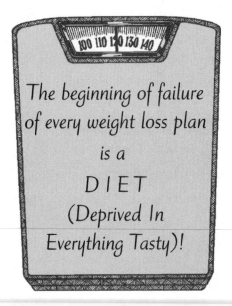

The beginning of failure of every weight loss plan is a

D I E T

(Deprived In Everything Tasty)!

If you think you must follow an eating plan that doesn't allow for savoring some excellent meals, or a plan that requires you to eat like a bird, you will find yourself feeling very deprived. The beginning of failure of every weight loss plan is a DIET (Deprived In Everything Tasty)!

This book is NOT about a DIET. It's about a lifestyle of health and vitality. It is about a program that allows you a life beyond extraordinary.

I can imagine by now that you are ready to scan ahead and find out what program I'm going to recommend.

✻ *How does it work?*

✻ *How much weight will I lose?*

✻ *How will I become as energized as the Energizer Bunny®?*

✻ *How fast will it happen?*

✻ *How painful will it be?*

I understand! I like to get to the point quickly in self-help books myself. In the next chapter, I will indulge your desires and get to the recommended program.

However, I hope you will read the entire book. Any program will work...for a while! I'm not interested in offering you a quick fix solution. I'm interested in seeing you make a lifelong change that will result in your desired weight loss, but also—more importantly—excellent health, abundant energy, and a radiance for life!

The eating program is only a minor piece of achieving this kind of life. (Remember, it's only 20 percent.) But I know you're eager to get started, so…here we go!

Chapter 3

What's the Program?

Research has shown the
single greatest predictor
of heart attack risk is
high levels of insulin.

I know you are eager to read a summary of the program in order to decide if you can live with it. Here is what I recommend:

Breakfast—High-protein meal

Snacks—High protein

Lunch—High-protein meal

Snacks—High protein

Dinner—Balanced meal with low-glycemic foods (also referred to as the 70-Minute Meal)

NO SNACKS AFTER DINNER

I'm ready for the onslaught of questions and comments...

But I only have time to grab a bagel in the morning.

What do you mean by high-protein meal?

I'll die if I can't have a snack before bedtime.

Why This Plan? How Does It Work?

I will devote the remainder of this chapter to answering both questions. I'll do my best to do it in simple, understandable terms because I think it's crucial that you understand what is happening in your body when you gain weight.

Sugar Is the Culprit

You've read about it in the news, you've heard about it on television talk shows. I'm here to confirm it for you: Sugar is the culprit!

And I'm not simply talking here about refined sugar! I'm talking about all the carbs that turn to sugar as soon as they begin the digestive process in your mouth, including potatoes, Cheetos™, pasta, bread, corn, rice—the list is a long one, and it encompasses many of the foods most common in the American diet.

How does this work? Let me address the biochemical process in a simple and entertaining manner. If you are a woman, chances are you understand much about the art of shopping. (And if you are a man, you might understand this analogy as the recipient of credit card bills.)

Let's imagine that you are at the mall. You have just found that perfect outfit that you have been searching for all day! Sure, it might cost a bit more than you intended to spend, but you've shopped all day, been to countless stores. Your feet are aching, so now you can justify the higher price.

You reach into your purse, pull out your wallet, and you find two things: a credit card and a deposit slip. Very clearly, if you want the outfit, the deposit slip serves no purpose.

However, if you are to reach your goal of saving enough money for the cruise for which you are buying the outfit, you should be making good use of the deposit slip. One is for spending money, one is for saving money. Each has a significant purpose.

So it is with two opposing hormones in our bodies. We have a "saving" hormone called insulin, and a "spending" hormone called glucagon.

In our bodies, we want to make excellent use of the "spending" hormone!

I knew you'd like this analogy. Spend! Spend! Spend! In my live seminars, participants receive a Glucagon Credit Card and an Insulin Deposit Slip to make the point. These items are pictured below.

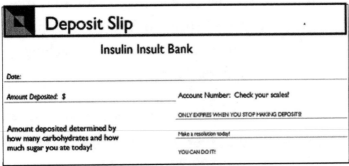

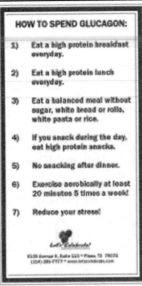

```
┌─────────────────────────────────────┐
│  CELEBRATION NATIONAL BANK           │
│  No spending limit on                │
│  GLUCAGON                            │
│                                      │
│  0112 0200 7777 7777   no expiration │
└─────────────────────────────────────┘
```

Insulin, the Saving Hormone

Insulin is a hormone created by our bodies by the pancreas. It is released when we eat carbohydrates (carbs) and sugar. Its primary responsibility is to carry glucose and fats into our body's cells for energy use.

So, when we eat sugar, starches, and high-carbohydrate foods, our body releases insulin (the "saving" hormone) to energize us AND to store excess glucose from our blood stream away in our fat cells for future use.

Insulin also increases our cravings for more carbohydrates. Have you ever just had to eat one more snack even when you knew you were already satisfied? That craving results from too much insulin in your blood stream.

Our body turns the carbs we've eaten into glucose (blood sugar). Then the job of insulin is to deliver the glucose wherever it is needed in the body for energy. In addition, if insulin senses that there is more glucose than it can deliver at the moment, it sends a message to the pancreas calling for more insulin and it sends a message to the liver to begin converting the excess glucose into triglycerides (a fancy word for fat in your blood).

Insulin (because it is such an excellent "saver") then begins its job of filling out deposit slips and "depositing" all that extra blood sugar into your fat cells, saving energy for a time when it is needed.

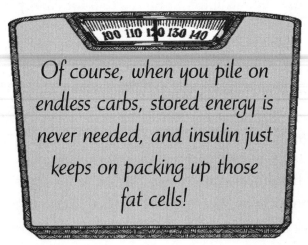

Of course, when you pile on endless carbs, stored energy is never needed, and insulin just keeps on packing up those fat cells!

You find yourself in a situation where you have plenty of glucose to use at the moment, and plenty to save. Sure, you've got an abundant "savings account," because you're full of fat! *(Oops...that's not what you really wanted in your savings account, is it?)*

When insulin is present in your blood in appropriate amounts, it's a very supportive hormone. It delivers energy to your cells and acts as a growth hormone for new cell growth.

However, when insulin is overabundant in the blood stream, it can wreak havoc on your health. Research has shown that insulin can activate various metabolic pathways, causing sleepiness, hunger, dizziness, bloating, elevated blood pressure and cholesterol levels, fluid retention, damage to arteries, coronary problems...just to mention a few of the potential problems (Reaven, 1997).

In fact, research has shown the single greatest predictor of heart attack risk is high levels of insulin. A study of thousands of fire fighters found that insulin levels were more significant in heart attack risk than smoking history, hereditary concerns, or exercise habits (AHA, 1998).

Excess insulin is an epidemic in our society, one that is wreaking havoc on our health! Still, we refuse to acknowledge its significance. I trust that you will take this matter seriously as we explore it further in the remainder of this book.

Glucagon, the Spending Hormone

Glucagon is our "spending" hormone. It is called into action when we need energy and there isn't enough available in the blood stream in the form of glucose.

Glucagon goes to the fat cells (with its credit card, which has UNLIMITED spending limits) and withdraws those "deposits" in order to "spend" them on rebuilding muscles and providing fuel. I feel certain you are way ahead of me here and may be thinking, "Okay, give me some glucagon pills." That sounds like an excellent idea, but it's not that simple!

When insulin is present in your system (the result of carbohydrate intake), it interrupts and prohibits the use of glucagon. So even if I created a glucagon pill, it would be rendered useless as long as you continued to spike insulin in your blood stream with your diet. If we can stop your insulin levels from spiking, you won't need glucagon pills anyway!

The situation is a lot like having a prepaid MasterCard® account with a $10 million credit, but you can never get to the store to spend it. And why can't you get to the store? Because your car (your blood chemistry) is on automatic pilot. Every time you get in it, it drives you straight to the bank to make a deposit, instead of to the mall to spend your credit balance.

Here is exactly what sugar and carbs do in your body: They put your body on automatic pilot, never letting you spend the fat, even when you don't eat that much. Automatic deposits are continually made to your fat cells.

Now I can imagine all the calls I will receive from folks: "How could you write an entire book telling us to go spend, spend, spend?" If we spent our fat through the use of glucacon the way we spend our money through the use of credit cards, we would not be a nation populated by obese people!

Hyperinsulinemia

I think it's crucial for you as my readers to fully comprehend the impact these conditions have on you, to be able to identify their symptoms, and to understand the role sugar and carb intake plays in them.

Hypoglycemia literally means "low blood sugar." Although it is generally used to identify a situation where there is not enough glucose (sugar) in the blood, it also occurs when there is too much insulin in the blood stream. Thus, it's also referred to as hyperinsulinemia.

How do we end up with too much insulin in the blood stream? Hyperinsulinemia often occurs when cells become resistant to insulin. It's a situation very similar to the fable of crying wolf. When we first hear the cries, we take them seriously and respond immediately. But when we've heard them time after time and responded, only to see that there's no real jeopardy, we eventually learn to disregard the call. We become immune to its effect.

When our bodies are first bombarded with insulin, the cells work overtime to process it and take it in. After the pattern has continually repeated itself, however, the cells become resistant to the onslaught, and therefore the insulin has no choice but to deliver the blood sugar to fat cells.

Because the blood sugar is carried into fat cells, as opposed to other cells that need it for rebuilding themselves, the body cries out for more insulin to be produced. The insulin released causes us to crave carbohydrates, and the cycle begins.

We eat more carbs; they are converted to blood sugar. The body releases insulin to deliver the blood sugar to cells. These cells are insulin-resistant, so the insulin delivers the blood sugar to fat cells. The body cries out for more blood sugar, more insulin is released, we crave carbs, we eat them...the cycle continues. Your weight goes up! Your body fat goes up! Your spirits go down!

Here are some of the common symptoms of hypoglycemia:

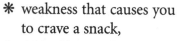

* weakness that causes you to crave a snack,
* difficulty focusing,
* sweating without physical exertion,
* heart pounding,
* anxiety or panic attacks,
* sluggishness,
* shakiness, and
* irritability.

These are just a few of the symptoms often associated with hypoglycemia or hyperinsulinemia.

As mentioned earlier, excess insulin in our system does more than cause weight gain. In addition,

It encourages the kidneys to retain salt and fluid; it stimulates the production of cholesterol by the liver; it fuels an increase in triglyceride production; it thickens the muscular portion of the artery walls, increasing the risk for high blood pressure; and it sends a strong message to the fat cells to store incoming sugar and fat. (Eades and Eades, 1996)

Bring on the Glucagon

From the example of "saving" (insulin) and "spending" (glucagon) above, we can see clearly that what we need is a strong, consistent release of glucagon. Not only does glucagon usher fat out of the cell, but it also counteracts some of the negative effects of too much insulin.

Glucagon sends signals to the kidneys to release excess salt and fluid, to the liver to slow down the production of cholesterol and triglycerides, to the artery wall to relax and drop blood pressure, and to the fat cells to release stored fat to be burned for energy. (Eades and Eades, 1996)

So how do you get the glucagons flowing? The most significant and efficient method of increasing the release of glucagon is to lower your carb intake.

Why Do I Have to Eat High Protein for the First Two Meals of the Day?

The primary reason for high protein intake for the first two meals of the day is to give your body the opportunity to pour on the glucagon. You give your body an opportunity to rest and recover from its normal "automatic pilot" onslaught of insulin, and glucagon gets a chance to "do its thing."

Let's take a look at the typical American way of eating. You get up in the morning and you are in a hurry. So you grab a bagel on the way out the door. *EEEEEEK!* (the sound of your insulin level screeching upward).

Naturally, your body dumps insulin to handle the carbohydrates, and for some strange reason you are craving something sweet by 10 a.m.

You head to the break room, and there it is! Someone brought in the food of the gods...Krispy Kreme Doughnuts™! And you need a little coffee to wake you up, so you pour yourself a cup and use a packet of Sweet 'N Low® to keep the calories down, then pour in two International Delight® Irish Créme coffee creamers (99 percent sugar)! *EEEEEEEK!* There goes that insulin skyrocketing again!

For lunch, you eat at your desk—a sandwich, a bag of chips, and a soft drink. *EEEEEEK!* There goes the insulin level...up and off the charts!

Then you are surprised when you can't shake the nap that keeps summoning you to drift away at your desk all afternoon. SO...what else could you do? You go to the break room and get a Snickers™, but to be good this time, you get a diet soft drink! *EEEEEEK!* There it goes again: Insulin awash in your blood stream as plentiful as water in the ocean!

For dinner, you vow to do better. You eat a baked potato with Molly McButter™, some corn, and a roll without butter. *EEEEEEK!*

You are loaded with insulin by now, but you can rest assured that the ice cream in the freezer will call your name while you're watching TV! *EEEEEEK!*

I didn't eat that much, but I keep gaining weight!

Understand what is most significant here:

 ✽It's *not* how much you eat.
 ✽It's *not* how many fat grams you consume.
 ✽ It *is* how much insulin you dump into your blood stream every day and how many times you do it.

You can eat your high-protein meals at any two meals of the day you prefer. I recommend that you consume high-protein meals earlier in the day because, as you can see by the examples above, once you begin dumping insulin into your system, stopping can be difficult.

In a seminar in South Dakota recently, a woman asked me if she could eat her balanced meal at breakfast instead of dinner. I explained why it was better if she had it for her last meal of the day. However, when I learned she worked the graveyard shift at the post office, I understood that breakfast was her last meal of the day!

Exactly How Much Protein Should I Eat?
Generally, you may eat protein to your heart's content, with the exception of milk. Although I recommend fish and fowl for those who are not vegetarian, you may eat any meat (preferably lean meat).

I find many people have digestive reactions to dairy products. If you aren't one of those people, you may eat dairy to your heart's content.

However, when you set out to eat protein, learn to read labels. Labels will tell you how much protein and how many carbohydrates the food contains. If you stay with those that have less than 1 gram (< 1) carbohydrate content, you will notice a remarkable difference.

You may eat bacon, rabbit, veal, beef, pastrami, sausage (without sugar), pork, venison, buffalo, chicken, Cornish hen, duck, goose, pheasant, turkey, fish and shellfish, eggs, egg substitutes, cream cheese, cottage cheese, limited milk, cream, half-and-half, sour cream, tofu, vegetarian meat alternatives, or other cheeses.

Why Is Protein So Important?

For our purposes, the most significant reason to consume protein is that it elicits absolutely no insulin response in your body. If there is no insulin, no fat is being stored away for future use! However, protein has many other health benefits for your body:

> Protein is an essential nutrient, crucial for repairing and maintaining muscles and connective tissue, regulating the body's water balance, producing key hormones and enzymes, and keeping a healthy immune system. (Applegate, 2001)

What Else Can I Eat for Breakfast and Lunch?

In addition to your protein for breakfast and lunch, you need to consume some high-protein veggies. In our country, we rarely eat vegetables with breakfast. In most other cultures, green vegetables are a vital part of the morning meal! Perhaps it's time to change a few traditions!

You need high-protein vegetables to keep fiber in your system. Although these high-protein vegetables contain moderate amounts of carbohydrates, they will not cause insulin dumps and they will keep your body from becoming overly sensitive to carbohydrates.

Here is the list from which you should make your vegetable selections for your two high-protein meals:

Alfalfa sprouts	Cucumbers	Okra
Artichokes	Green beans	Parsley
Asparagus	Green or red	Radishes
Bean sprouts	peppers	Scallions
Broccoli	Greens	Snap beans
Cabbage	Kale	Spinach
Cauliflower	Lettuce	
Celery	Mushrooms	

I highly recommend a Caesar salad with your lunch meal, but I caution you to read the label on your packaged dressing. Many brands on the market are high in protein, and several have no carbohydrate content whatsoever. However, many of the low-fat and fat-free dressings have added sugar. (Didn't you ever wonder what made them so tasty after they removed the fat content?) **You are not nearly so concerned with the fat content as you are with the sugar/carbohydrate content!**

I know you may think you cannot possibly make it between meals without some snacks! For snacks and extras, I recommend:

Veggies with Caesar dip
Celery stick stuffed with cream cheese
Pork rinds
Boiled egg
Black olives
Green olives (without the pimentos)
Dill pickles
Garlic
Anything from the lists of vegetables, meat, and dairy products above
You may season your snacks with salt (preferably sea salt) and pepper
You're welcome to use mayonnaise (not light or fat-free) and mustard

One More Thing About Snacks

If you are a between-meal snacker, you must keep your snacks high in protein. With Sam's Club warehouse and Costco in most large cities, you can pick up bags of frozen chicken breasts, drumsticks, or wings that are fully cooked. Throw them into the microwave for 10 seconds, and voilà! You have a nutritious snack! (One more time: Read the labels. Some foods may be coated with sugar-laden sauces.)

In the *Companion Guide,* you will find some of my high-protein recipes. I highly encourage preparing these recipes in large quantities, putting them in freezer containers, and popping them in the microwave when you have a snack attack.

For those of you who simply cannot bear to be without popcorn while you are watching television in the evening, a similar microwave preparation is now available for "popping" your own pork rinds!

What About Protein Bars and Beverage Meal Replacements?

Currently, I have found no bars or beverages on the market that I highly recommend. My surface mail and email boxes are stuffed with package wrappers or information copied from them on a continuous basis.

Each message asks me if "this one" is acceptable outside the 70-minute meal. All these queries teach me that meal replacements in both bar and drink form are in high demand.

In the near future, I will develop my own bars and beverage meal replacements. In the meantime, my best advice to you is this: Read labels!

If a product contains more than 2 grams of carbohydrates per serving, stay away from it. If each serving is under the 2-gram limit (and even that amount will cause a small insulin spike), consuming such a food is certainly better than visiting a drive-through window and munching down a cheeseburger (unless, of course, you remove the bun and eat only the meat and cheese). Ideally, you want products that contain no sugar grams.

Some powders on the market boast 100 percent protein. Close examination of the label, however, reveals a high number of carbohydrates per serving. If you manage to find one with no carbs and no sugars, the taste is probably nasty, and the manufacturer will likely recommend that you mix the powder with milk or fruit juice. Both of these mixers are 70-minute commodities.

I'll offer this quick tip from my own experience: If you find an acceptable protein powder, put it in the blender with a few ice cubes, and use Diet Hansen's™ Black Cherry as the mixer. You'll find the result much more palatable than plain water, and you won't need to use milk or juice outside the 70-minute window.

Then I Can "Pig Out" at Dinner, Right?

Wrong! You cannot "pig out" at dinner. However, you may have a balanced meal of protein, fiber, and vegetables. You may have any vegetables and fiber foods you desire, with the exception of forbidden foods that will be discussed in the next chapter. You may have fish, fowl, meat, fruits and vegetables, and whole-grain products (whole-grain bread or rolls, whole-wheat pasta, whole-wheat crackers, etc.).

You may eat until you are fully satisfied. However, bingeing is a lifestyle you must leave behind. Most of us learn to binge when we have been deprived or when we are eating to meet emotional needs. (I'll have more to say about bingeing and eating to satisfy emotional needs in a later chapter.)

What About Fruit?

Fruit is one of those treat foods that must be saved for your 70-minute meal. (See *Why 70 Minutes?*

below.) Fruit contains many  phytochemicals that have great health benefits. I wrote an entire book addressing the benefits that you might find helpful. It's entitled *Designing Your Life with Designer Foods: The Facts About Phytochemicals.*

The natural sugars contained in fruit still cause a rise in your insulin, however, and for that reason all fruit and fruit juices must be consumed during your 70-minute meal.

When you're going to consume fruit, eat it at the beginning of your 70 minutes, prior to any other foods. Fruit eaten on top of other foods tends to cause indigestion (Diamond and Schnell, 1996).

What About Alcohol?

I hope that if you consume alcohol, you do so in moderation. Certainly a glass of wine with dinner has been shown to be heart-healthy (Schlienger, 2001) and possibly a cancer preventive (CNN.com, 2000). However, all alcohol is sugar-laden, and its consumption must occur during the 70-minute meal.

Why 70 Minutes?

You may be wondering, "Why is it that I can eat foods during this meal that I cannot eat during the day?" This is an excellent question, and I want you to fully understand the answer. When you grasp this concept, you'll be motivated to eat more healthily for the rest of your life!

I've already mentioned that insulin is released when we ingest carbohydrates. When we allow our bodies a 12- to 24-hour rest period between insulin releases, insulin levels normalize in the blood stream (Heller et al., 1999).

The truth is, most of us don't have a clue how it might feel to experience a normalized insulin level, because **most of us have never lived more than six to eight hours without maxing out on carbohydrates**— and that's only when we sleep! We go to bed with carbs (popcorn while watching TV, or that last bowl of ice cream), and we wake up to carbs (bagels, cereal, hash browns, pancakes).

Let's get back to how insulin releases occur in our bodies. When we ingest food, insulin is released in two phases. The first phase is released when we begin to eat carbohydrates. The amount released is preset, depending on the amount of carbohydrates you normally ingest. If you normally ingest large quantities of carbs, your body expects you to do the same and dumps a huge supply of insulin into your blood stream, ready to carry that glucose to the cells for energy and store the rest in your fat cells.

The second release of insulin occurs about 75 to 85 minutes after your first bite of carbohydrates. The extent of this second release depends on how long you continue to eat carbohydrates at that meal. **If you have completed your carbohydrate eating within the 75- to 85-minute period, no additional insulin is released.**

You can see how carbohydrates can be eaten at this meal, because if you eat high-protein meals during the day, your body won't have its first real insulin release until this time. And, as long as you keep the time period for eating carbohydrates under 70 minutes (to be safe), you will not produce a second dose of insulin, with its cravings and havoc for your health.

For those of you who are already searching for "loopholes" in the plan, you may be thinking, "Well, I guess that means I can eat ANYTHING I want during that 70 minutes!"

Well—truly—if you just must "cheat," the 70-minute period is the time to do it! If you must have a brownie, do it in the 70-minute time period. If you must have a baked potato, do it within that time.

However, remember this: The more carbohydrates you consume—and particularly those illegal carbs (most things that are white and full of sugar)—the more difficulty your body will face in normalizing your insulin dump.

Your metabolism will memorize your high carb consumption and dump much more insulin than is needed into your system. Your savings account of fat will flourish!

This is a situation that I refer to as "insulin insult." Your body is deteriorating because of the continuing insults of insulin.

Certainly, a treat consumed on a special occasion won't ruin your entire program! Then when you do have a special treat, your body won't overreact.

I have a client who was certain he could not live without potatoes. He didn't care how they were prepared; he was a Midwest farm boy and "you are just supposed to have potatoes with every meal, that's all there is to it!"

I suggested that he commit to 30 days without potatoes, then add them back into his 70-minute meal in moderation. During the 30-day period without potatoes, he lost 21 pounds, and when the big day came for reintroducing potatoes to his diet, he had forgotten about it altogether until I reminded him!

He now eats potatoes at one of his 70-minute meals weekly, and he has continued his weight loss (although at a slower rate). So if you think you can't live without a forbidden food, give your body an opportunity to normalize its insulin dumps for 30 days, then add it back moderately.

After you've eaten this way for a time, your body begins to regulate the amount of insulin it produces, and your metabolic system returns to normal. The results?

* You will not feel sluggish.
* You will not have day and night sweats.
* Glucagon will begin working on your behalf and you will notice weight and fat loss.
* Your blood pressure and cholesterol should decrease.
* Your glucose levels should decrease.
* You will have more energy.
* You will feel less irritable.
* You will have a more positive outlook on life.

Is anyone interested in claiming that list for themselves? I, for one, desire EVERYTHING on the list!

This is not a diet. This is a way of eating. **No measuring. No portion control. No counting. No starving.**

I believe you can live this way, and when the results come you will be motivated to continue!

Here's a little story that might inspire you to get started. Gary had been battling with fatigue and energy problems for years because of a pituitary tumor. He described his condition to me with great sadness one day: "You know, it's worse than being tired. Much worse. It's like I'm out of gas. It's like I can't really get on my feet again. I guess I'll just have to get used to it."

My response: "You can get used to it or change it!" He sarcastically responded, "Yeah, right!"

I briefly explained the above outline to him and asked him to give it an honest try for just 10 days. He said, "Okay, I can do it for 10 days, but if it doesn't work, that's it!"

Within 10 days, his blood pressure was down; his blood sugar was down; his weight was down. More importantly, his energy and his spirits were up! Yours will be, too!

Are you willing to give it a 10-day try?

Chapter 4

Sugar is the Culprit

I was truly astounded when my studies revealed that sugar is more addictive than alcohol or nicotine.

B y now you are probably wondering...

What can I really eat?

How much?

When?

Let's talk specifically about what foods to eat at which meals and which foods to avoid altogether.

Sugar

Surely you are not going to ask me to give up sugar altogether, are you?

Well, yes. As a matter of fact, I *am* going to ask you to give up sugar altogether. And believe it or not, it won't kill you. **As a matter of fact, giving up sugar could save your life!**

Average Americans consume the equivalent of 35 teaspoons of sugar each day, totaling 130 pounds of sugar consumption each year!

You say, "I don't think *I* eat that much!" But think again: Sugar is in virtually everything. It's in the creamer you put in your coffee; it's in ketchup, soup, peanut butter, yogurt, salad dressings.

And we haven't even addressed desserts!

Most 12-ounce cans of cola beverages contain 17 teaspoons of sugar. When you understand the many hidden sources of sugar in your diet, you might be surprised by the total amount you consume.

I have an experience to relate about sugar consumption from my personal history. More than 15 years ago, I was working with addicts at an inpatient treatment center. Because the body metabolizes sugar in much the same way it metabolizes alcohol, we required that all addicts be placed on a sugar-free diet.

One day in mid-October, two of our patients, both young men, approached the desk where I was writing case notes and began moaning about my dietary restrictions. You would have thought I'd put them on a two-week fast.

"You don't know how hard it is!" they protested. "This just isn't fair!" And, "You could never survive if you had to eat this way!"

Because most of them stayed an average of two weeks, I responded, "I'll make a deal with you: Just stop the whining and follow the plan, and I promise you that while you're here I will not eat one bite of sugar!"

The two patients knew such a promise would be a challenge for me because I was famous for coming on the ward with a diet soft drink in one hand and a chocolate bar in the other. They always laughed and challenged me, "Why bother with a diet drink if you're going to eat a candy bar with it?"

They liked the idea of me sharing their deprivation, so they agreed to my proposal. For my part, I thought I'd benefit from seeing what it was really like for them to go "sugar-free," even though I was not an addict.

Or so I thought. By my third day without sugar, I had the shakes. I wanted candy so bad I would have crawled across town on my hands and knees on the hot pavement to get it!

Finally, the truth dawned on me: I was an addict, a sugar addict! I was truly astounded when my studies revealed that sugar is more addictive than alcohol or nicotine. Although I've never been intoxicated or smoked anything at all, I have worked with hundreds of people who were addicted to one or both of these substances, and now I was feeling many of the same sensations they described during their withdrawals!

By the end of the first week, something interesting happened. My nagging headaches stopped. The afternoon nap that crawled up on my shoulder every day didn't raise its head at all. I had more energy! I was less irritable! I was amazed!

Still, I was ready for the two-week period to end...but there was one small dilemma.

One of the patients to whom I had made the promise stayed on for six more weeks! How dare he? I had to keep my word, and I missed a whole holiday season of treats.

My mother is the queen of fabulous desserts. On every counter, on every end table, on every refrigerator shelf, there were treats to die for! Cookie cake, pecan pie, chocolate cake, peanut brittle, Martha Washington truffles, Rice Krispies® bars, peanut butter fudge, and everything homemade.

But I had made a promise, and I had to keep it. What a holiday. No fudge, no lemon icebox pie, no pecan pie, no divinity, no truffles. Somehow I lived through it, and I have remained sugar-free ever since!

As a matter of fact, when I told my mother before heading home for the holidays that I would not be partaking of her delicious treats (and the reason why), she began the tradition of sugar-free desserts that we have created through the years. You'll find recipes for them included in the *Companion Guide.* I often serve desserts to dinner guests, and when they see me eating them myself they will often say, "Oh, I thought you didn't eat sugar." When I respond that the dessert is sugar-free, they are always amazed.

I challenge you: Decide to learn to eat without sugar. You will find it difficult at first, but I promise you that I no longer miss it or crave it. There are countless sugar-free treats available!

Sugar's Evil Twin...Forbidden Foods
You mean I have to give up more than sugar?

Yes. I'm sorry to inform you that there are other forbidden foods! But don't stop reading. There are great alternatives for EVERYTHING you will give up!

Actually, the list is fairly short and easy to remember. Here are the foods that you must avoid because they immediately convert to sugar in the digestive process, which begins in your mouth. Here is the list:

> Sugar
> White grain products (white bread, white
>   rice)
> Potatoes
> Beets
> Carrots
> Corn
> Pasta

You might be thinking, "This leaves me NOTHING to eat!" Not so!

Instead of white bread, eat whole-wheat or whole-grain bread. Instead of white rice, eat whole-grain or brown rice. The list of vegetable substitutes for potatoes, beets, carrots, and corn is extensive: sweet potatoes, mushrooms, lentils, olives, green beans, peas, artichokes, broccoli, spinach, asparagus. Below you'll find a table offering suggested substitutions.

Suggested Substitutes for Forbidden Foods

Forbidden Foods	Suggested Substitutes
Potatoes	Sweet potatoes, lentils, wax beans, mushrooms, artichokes, spinach, asparagus, peas, green beans, olives
Potato chips	Pork rinds
White rice	Whole-grain rice
Pasta	Whole-grain pasta
White bread and rolls	Whole-grain bread and rolls
Sugar	Splenda™ (sucralose)

Sugar Substitutes

Many sugar substitutes are available today. Although there is great controversy on both sides of the aspartame debate, I prefer to avoid extensive use of products containing this substance.

I recommend instead the artificial sweetener Splenda™ (sucralose), which has been used for quite some time in Canada and Europe, but which has only recently been approved for use in the U.S. Splenda™ first appeared on the market in Ocean Spray's light juices (Lite Cran-Grape™, Lite Cran-Raspberry™, etc.). Recently, Diet Rite™ Cola and Diet RC™ have introduced Splenda™ as their sweetener. It is also available in bulk and packets in the sugar aisles of most grocery stores. It measures just like sugar.

Splenda™ is unique because the body does not metabolize it; it contains no calories and very little carbohydrate. It can be used in baking, as well as for sweetening drinks.

Are There Other Reasons to Give up Sugar?

In America, we consume unbelievable amounts of sugar.

We are given our first invitation to sugar addiction while on the nursing bottle. Most baby formulas still contain large amounts of sugar.

After we're weaned from the bottle, sugar serves as a reward. "Do all of your school work and we will have some cookies and a Coke™."

As teens we begin socializing. A typical Friday night at a friend's house consists of pizza, cupcakes, and soft drinks. As adults, the easiest snack is sugar: We pick up a bag of cookies; we keep candy kisses in a jar on our desks; we grab a donut on the way to work.

Yet sugar can be just as addictive as drugs, and just as dangerous to our health as carcinogens! Let's take a look at what research has shown us about problems and maladies created by sugar intake.

Research has shown that sugar intake is correlated with irregular, painful, and extremely uncomfortable menstrual cycles (Lorenc, 1972). Coronary disease and diabetes have been linked to sugar intake (Duffy, 1975). Sugar has been indicated in hyperactivity and poor academic performance in school (Goldman et al., 1986).

Sugar has been named as the cause in some sleep disorders, particularly difficulty falling asleep and difficulty staying asleep. Nagging headaches, allergies, and difficulties in concentration have also been linked to sugar intake (Appleton, 2002).

Loss of sexual desire is another result of sugar intake (Kennedy, 1999). We often blame our lack of desire on our partner or the aging process. In reality, there is considerable evidence that sugar is the culprit!

Coronary disease, hypertension, and diabetes have all been linked to sugar intake (Fontbonne et al., 1991, Fuh et al., 1987, Gwinup et al., 1991).

Here are some of the other maladies, conditions, and diseases that have been linked to sugar consumption:

cancer,
cystic fibrosis,
multiple sclerosis,
psoriasis,
asthma,
osteoporosis,
tooth decay,
inflammatory bowel disease,
arthritis,
chronic Candida infection,
intestinal gas,
canker sores,
gallstones,
constipation, and
chronic stomach upset (Kennedy, 2002).

Another source contributes additional sugar-related ailments to the list:

> weakened immune system,
> mood swings,
> liver enlargement,
> indigestion,
> edema,
> cataracts,
> acne,
> appendicitis,
> nearsightedness, and
> binge eating (Gittleman, 1996).

One researcher has tapped sugar as the source of all other addictions:

> Sugar addiction is the underlying addiction to all addictions. This includes smoking, drugs, alcohol, caffeine, certain foods including the sugar & [sic] high-glycemic carbohydrates & [sic] can even be seen in such addictions as gambling & [sic] shopping. It is also often very connected to anxiety-panic disorder, depression, sleep disorder, as well as all compulsions & [sic] addictive behaviors. (Bohorquez, 2001)

For years, I have encouraged clients struggling with anxiety and depression to eliminate sugar. Almost 100 percent of those who complied experienced significant reductions in those and other mood disorders simply by eliminating sugar from their diets.

The bottom line is this: You can break the sugar habit, and when you do, you'll be healthier. You will feel more energetic, and you will find a new zest for life. I challenge you to try it for 10 days!

Chapter 5

But I Crave Carbohydrates

I have also learned, through
many years of working with
eating-disordered individuals,
that overcoming a food addiction
offers a greater challenge than
overcoming a substance addiction.

I am constantly asked if I think there is any merit to the notion that some of us are "carbohydrate addicts." ABSOLUTELY! Because you're reading this book, chances are you can join our ranks!

However, I prefer not to use the phrase "carbohydrate addict" because of the mindset many of us have about addictions. We tend to think that an addiction is impossible to overcome, holding us hostage to eating carbohydrates and being fat the rest of our lives.

Many of my friends who have been clean and sober for years as a result of attending and working the program of Alcoholics Anonymous would be glad to tell you that there is hope for recovery from addiction. Not only is there hope, but there is a new and fulfilling life waiting for you.

I have also learned, through many years of working with eating-disordered individuals, that overcoming a food addiction offers a greater challenge than overcoming a substance addiction. After all, the addict can leave alcohol and drugs behind, but we must face food every day.

For these reasons, I prefer to address the situation as a *craving* for carbohydrates. By whatever name we call the syndrome, the facts are the same.

Am I a Carb Craver?

You can determine if you are a craver by taking the following little test.

Place a check beside each of the statements below that applies to you. Check if they *usually* apply to you. Then circle the points following the statement. This exercise is for no one except yourself, so be honest. Facing the problem is always half the battle!

____ When I eat a full breakfast, I notice that I am hungrier before lunch time than I am if I only drink coffee for breakfast. (6 points)

____ I find that I get tired and/or hungry in the middle of the afternoon. (2 points)

____ I become tired and sluggish after I eat a large meal. (1 point)

____ I sometimes put off evening plans or events because I lose my motivation after dinner. (4 points)

____ I have more difficulty stopping when I start eating junk food, sweets, and starches than I have with not eating at all. (5 points)

____ Around two hours after eating, I find that I experience one or more of the following: tiredness, hunger, irritability, shakiness, disorientation, lack of motivation, or head aches. Sometimes a snack alleviates those symptoms. (3 points)

____ Stress throws me into a desire for a snack. (3 points)

____ Foods with sugar and/or artificial sweeteners are included in most of my meals. (1 point)

____ As I age, I tend to gain weight more easily.(3 points)

____ At least one of my close relatives is overweight.

(3 points)

____ My lifestyle isn't very active.   (3 points)

____ I experience stress at work and/or home fairly

regularly.   (3 points)

____ I have one or more of the following: high blood

pressure, high cholesterol, high triglycerides, or

adult-onset diabetes.   (5 points)

____ One or both of my parents have experienced the

following: high blood pressure, high cholesterol,

high triglycerides, adult-onset diabetes, heart disease,

atherosclerosis, vascular disease, or stroke.(4 points)

____ I take any of the following regularly: female hormone

replacement therapy, stool softeners, or medication

for high blood pressure, high cholesterol, high

triglycerides, adult-onset diabetes, water retention,

heartburn, or indigestion.   (4 points)

TOTAL YOUR CIRCLED POINTS: _____

Adapted from the *Carbohydrate Addict's LifeSpan
Quiz* (Heller and Heller, 1998)

WHAT DOES THE SCORE MEAN?

If you have 13 or fewer points, you are either naturally thin or you were not totally honest.

If you have 14 to 22 points, you are a mild craver and you are affected by insulin insult.

If you have 23 to 35 points, you are a moderate craver and are seriously affected by insulin insult.

If you have 36 to 50 points, you are a strong craver and have major problems with insulin insult; there is a high probability that you have high blood pressure, adult-onset diabetes, depression anxiety, or major weight problems.

No matter where you scored, the eating plan outlined in this book will probably bring you the results you desire. Individuals scoring between 23 and 50 points, however, *need* to follow this plan, not only for weight loss and energy increase, but for general health purposes and for quality of life.

This eating program is designed to address the root cause of weight problems and lack of energy. It addresses the insulin and metabolic imbalances that could be creating disorders in your body without your awareness.

Ultimately, we are encompassing more than weight loss with this approach. We're addressing your health, the quality of your life, your longevity. We want to enable you to enjoy every step of your journey through life!

Chapter 6

Eating to Change Your Life and Your Health

I want to help you take care
of your body the way you
would take care of a loved
one who was ill.

I know that most of you are reading this book to address weight issues. Nothing else may seem to matter other than losing that excess weight! If you are feeling that way right now, I completely understand.

One of my goals in creating this program, however, is to help you care so much about yourself by the time you finish this book that weight is only a secondary concern.

Many women and some men tend to have a "take care of" gene. We "take care of" the kids. We "take care of" the crises in the neighborhood. We "take care of" the needs of ailing loved ones. The list goes on, but all too often we put ourselves at the bottom of that list—if we even include ourselves on the list at all.

Nothing would make me happier than to learn that as a result of reading this book, you put yourself at the top of the list (just below your faith) and that you care about your health more than your weight.

Invincible

As I was growing up, I thought I was invincible. I remember as a teenager I wanted to lose some of my baby fat, and my Aunt Mamie told me about a high-protein gram-counting diet. I decided to try it, and boy did it ever work for me! I dropped weight like crazy!

One of my teachers at school (who—believe me!—needed to be on the diet) asked me how I lost weight. I told her and she gave me this huge lecture about how dangerous that diet was and how it would ruin my liver and gall bladder and who-knows-what else.

I remember my unspoken responses to her as she lectured me, "You know, if you were on this diet, it would probably do all those awful things to you, but none of those things will happen to me!" Although much of what she was referring to was indeed a myth,

I refused to concern myself the least bit because I really believed I was invincible.

I think as a young person, I just assumed that I would live forever. It never dawned on me that gravity would take effect at some point and that cellulite was no respecter of persons.

I received a great email recently about the wonder of the aging process.

> My thighs were stolen from me during the night a few years ago. It was just that quick. I went to sleep in my body and woke up with someone else's thighs. The new ones had the texture of cooked oatmeal.

> Who could have done such a cruel thing to legs that had been wholly, if imperfectly, mine for years? Whose thighs were these? What happened to mine?

> I spent the entire summer looking for them. I searched, in vain, at pools and beaches, anywhere I might find female limbs exposed. I became obsessed.

> I had nightmares filled with cellulite and flesh that turns to bumps in the night. Finally, hurt and angry, I resigned myself to living out my life in jeans and Sheer Energy™ pantyhose.

> Then, just when my guard was down, the thieves struck again. My rear end was next. I knew it was

the same gang, because they took pains to match my new rear end (although badly attached at least three inches lower than the original) to the thighs they had stuck me with earlier. Now my rear complemented my legs, lump for lump. Frantic, I prayed that long skirts would stay in fashion.

Two years ago I realized my arms had been switched. One morning while fixing my hair, I watched, horrified but fascinated, as the flesh of my upper arms swung to and fro with the motion of the hairbrush.

What could they do to me next? Age? Age had nothing to do with it. Age was supposed to creep up, unnoticed and intangible, something like maturity.

NO, I was being attacked, repeatedly and without warning. That's why I've decided to share my story. I can't take on the medical profession by myself.

Women of America, wake up and smell the coffee! That isn't really "plastic" those surgeons are using. You know where they're getting those replacement parts, don't you? The next time you suspect someone has had a face "lifted," look again! Was it lifted from you?

Check out those tummy tucks and buttocks raisings. Look familiar? Are those your eyelids on that movie star? I think I finally may have found my thighs...and I hope that Cindy Crawford paid a really good price for them!

Time and reminders like this one have helped me set aside my youthful feeling of invincibility.

I hope that you are in such good health you've had no need to face serious physical concerns. If you have had such issues, I want to help you take care of your body the way you would take care of a loved one who was ill. If you have warning signs that you are at risk, I want to help you remove all risks and achieve optimal health. This large objective sums up my hoped-for outcome for this book and my heart's desire for you!

Why Is Insulin So Potentially Dangerous?

Most of us first hear of insulin when we learn that someone is diabetic. We learn that insulin injections balance the diabetic's glucose levels, potentially making their lives fairly normal. Logically, we classify insulin in our minds as a "good guy."

Certainly, insofar as our bodies need insulin, it is a "good guy." I've pointed out in earlier chapters, however, that excessive insulin is often the cause of high blood pressure, high triglycerides (fat in the blood), weight gain, atherosclerosis, peripheral vascular diseases, and heart disease.

We remember that insulin is a hormone secreted by the pancreas for the metabolism of carbohydrates.

Sounds pretty benign, right? Then how is it that such a benign hormone can cause such major problems in the body?

I'm sure you have heard the little joke about the difference between going hormonal and going postal: At least when you went postal, you had mail to deliver.

Actually, I never mind the female hormone jokes. When I hear them (and why do men always seem to be the ones telling them?), I simply make a true statement: I find it totally amazing that when estrogen gets low and our testosterone levels rise, we act like men, and people find it distasteful.

Insulin is one hormone that affects both men and women similarly. It serves the very crucial role in our bodies of providing energy to our muscles so that they can repair themselves and function properly. It provides fuel to the nervous system and keeps our vital organs nourished. When insulin is present in our bodies at appropriate and balanced levels, it is certainly a *good guy.*

When insulin takes over, however, we are at risk for all of the diseases and concerns listed above. Let me mention again that aside from the other serious health threats excess insulin poses, insulin insult begins packing our fat cells to the point of bulging!

The Helsinki Policeman Study

A 22-year study of policemen in Helsinki was one of the first to link hyperinsulinemia to the risk of cardiac disease. Researchers followed 970 policemen, ages 34 to 64, who were free of heart disease at the beginning of the study. They found that hyperinsulinemia (too much insulin in the blood stream) was the single greatest predictor of coronary heart disease risk (Pyorala et al., 1998). After reviewing the medical literature on related topics, another scientist stated, "The relation of insulin resistance to cardiovascular risk particularly for coronary artery disease has been well established in many prospective studies" (Haffner, 1999).

When Insulin Reigns

When insulin reigns in our system, not only do we have health concerns, but we also have a real battle with controlling our food consumption. Insulin has been shown to do three things:

1) It heightens the tastes of foods, making some of them taste sweeter.
2) It increases the amount of food we want to eat.
3) It causes recurring cravings for carbohydrates.

    Let's look at each of these factors individually.

1) It heightens the tastes of foods, making some of them taste sweeter.

When overabundant insulin is present in your system, carbohydrates simply taste better. Have you ever had this experience? You know that you've eaten enough, that you are totally satisfied, but what you are eating seems unbelievably delicious and you simply don't want to stop eating it. This sensation is a good indicator that there is too much insulin in your system at the time.

Shortly after I learned this concept, I was presented with a great example in my own life. We were eating out at my daughter's favorite Italian restaurant. She had a caramel chocolate cheesecake for dessert. She was so full that she was literally holding her stomach. I suggested that she take her cheesecake home for later. She answered by insisting that she had to eat it then. After a few more bites, she agreed and asked for a carry-out container.

The next afternoon, she pulled the leftover cheesecake from the refrigerator. As she was eating it, I asked her if it was heavenly. Her response was interesting: "It's pretty good, but not nearly as good as I thought it was last night." I found it illuminating that my daughter thought the cheesecake tastiest when a meal of pasta and white bread had flooded her system with insulin.

2) It increases the amount of food we want to eat.

When you eat a meal that is high in carbohydrates or a meal that lasts longer than 70 minutes, your body releases a second dump of insulin into the system. This insulin creates cravings for more food, and food intake is increased.

I experienced an example of this phenomenon during a trip to Sweden. I was visiting with a fine gentleman who held rights to a nutritional product I wanted to bring to America. Following a day of meetings, he invited me to dinner with a physician friend and himself.

We went to a restaurant where the menu was written in Swedish, so I trusted him to order for me. First came a very small salad. It was in a very small bowl less than three inches wide containing a few pieces of lettuce and an interesting sauce. About 10 minutes later, a cup of broth with mushrooms arrived in a bowl of similar size. About 10 minutes later, another bowl appeared containing noodles and a creamy sauce.

I remember thinking, "Well, I guess this is it. I hope the hotel has room service." After more chat, my companions explained to me that Swedes begin the meal this way in order to "work up your appetite" for the meal to come.

Soon another small bowl arrived, this time filled with potatoes. Finally, a platter of food arrived that was enough to serve my entire family, an astonishing amount of food including a nice piece of broiled fish, a corn soufflé, a stuffing-like dish, a mixture of vegetables, and shrimp au gratin.

I found myself eating more than I had thought myself capable of consuming! When the first dessert came, I explained that I did not eat sugar, and everyone else set about consuming the lovely pastries the server had brought. Then came a second dessert, followed closely by a third and final one.

Here is a classic example of insulin-driven food intake, and certainly an experience that I will never forget!

3) It causes recurring cravings for carbohydrates.

Once the cycle of craving for carbohydrates begins, it never lets up. When we continue to eat carbs, our pancreas dumps more and more insulin into the system. As the cells become resistant to the onslaught of insurgent insulin, the hormone remains trapped in the blood stream, creating further cravings for carbohydrates. As we eat more carbs, even more insulin is dumped into the system. The endless cycle begins. If this situation is sustained long enough, adult-onset diabetes begins.

Keep Yourself from Disease

I mentioned in an earlier chapter all of the diseases, conditions, and maladies for which we are at risk when we flood our systems with insulin. I fully understand that we find it very difficult to take disease seriously until it hits us very close to home, and so I think an analogy drawn from life might make the dangers more immediate and accessible for us.

If we ignored our jobs and treated them as carelessly as we treat our bodies, many of us would find ourselves unemployable. We would never think of finding a major problem in our department at work and turning our back on it. We would never think of blatantly displaying behaviors that would cause demotion.

Quite often, however, we treat our own bodies in just these ways. Perhaps we all think we are invincible. I know many diabetics who "pop their little pills" and continue to eat carbohydrates as if there were no issue. I have attempted to explain to many of them that the medication might stabilize their blood sugar for the moment, but they are setting themselves up for the potentially serious long-term side effects of diabetes, such as blindness, amputations, even death.

I plead with you to take this message seriously. I plead with you to take care of your body and your health. An old advertisement touted the phrase: "You only go around once." Make the best of it!

Chapter 7

The Psychology of Weight Loss and Outstanding Health

You will find yourself more motivated to avoid things you consider painful than you will be to embrace things that you deem pleasurable.

Why include this chapter in a book about weight loss? Simply because success with weight loss is 20 percent about a plan and 80 percent about your psychology. I can provide you with the greatest plan in the world, but if your psychology isn't addressed, no plan will work for you.

You might achieve temporary success, but the long-term effects would be disappointing. I am committed to your long-term success, and I know this material is essential for you to achieve the results you desire, the results you deserve!

Our Dance with Pain and Pleasure

You must first understand our dance with pain and pleasure before you begin your journey to lose weight, revitalize your energy, or master excellent health.

Simply put: We will do more to pass up pain than we will do to pursue pleasure. You may be thinking, "That sounds totally crazy." Indeed it does! But it is also very true.

This means you will find yourself more motivated to avoid things you consider painful than you will be to embrace things that you deem pleasurable.

For example, we often tell children that they must complete their homework before they can go out to play. Those youngsters who don't like homework find themselves squirming, daydreaming, doodling, and shuffling papers. Why? They are more motivated to pass up the homework they consider painful than they are to get it over with so they can go out to play (pleasure).

You've seen it in yourself. You are invited to a party that you don't care to attend. The party is scheduled for the only night of the week when you could stay home and rest. However, you do not want to "hear it" from your friend if you don't go, so you get dressed and go. You are more motivated to avoid the pain of your friend's protest than you are to stay home and rest (pleasure).

Recently, a friend of mine went to a workshop at a treatment center in Arizona. Although his purpose was to learn to set appropriate boundaries in his life, his class had participants from the inpatient portion of the center as well.

During one of the exercises, the facilitator was explaining the three A's: acknowledging, acceptance, and action. One of the inpatient participants with an eating disorder explained that he acknowledged he had a problem, he accepted that it was a problem, but he was having difficulty taking action.

While my friend watched, the facilitator spent the next few hours working with this man, attempting to help him take action. My friend and I had participated in a coaching program the year before that fully explained the impact of the dance with pain and pleasure. He asked the facilitator if he could provide some feedback.

When the facilitator agreed, my friend turned to the man with the problem and said, "You know, either you are still getting some benefits out of your eating disorder, or perhaps you have so much pain attached to changing it that you keep yourself paralyzed."

Tearfully, the man admitted that he had received more concerned attention from his wife since his eating disorder emerged. He acknowledged that he also could not imagine the horror of having to learn to eat normally again! My friend asked him to name three other ways he could achieve intimacy with his wife, and to talk about how amazing he would feel if he began eating appropriately. The facilitator was astonished as the patient finally began to design his action steps.

We often tend to look for deep psychological reasons for our choices and for the situations in which we find ourselves when we could often resolve our issues simply by addressing our dance with pain and pleasure.

What Does This Have to Do with Weight Loss?

You must design your program so that your dance with pain and pleasure works for you. You've often heard that "it's all in your head!" Actually, there is some truth to that.

Things only mean what you decide that they mean. For example, when I was running my outpatient treatment center, we had lunches catered daily. Because of the variety of dietary requirements, the meals were delivered individually packaged, and those with special dietary needs were marked by first name. Because I did not eat sugar, I ordered a special lunch for myself.

Day after day, my lunch arrived dripping in sugar-laden barbecue sauce, or with desserts. After this had happened for several days, I had my assistant call the catering company and ask them to correct the situation. The next day when the food was delivered, all the meals were marked as usual in small black print, with one exception. My lunch was marked in large red letters.

I laughed and thought, "Well, I suppose that is their way of apologizing." My assistant had a different opinion. She felt the caterer was mocking her call and our request that my dietary requirements be met. She found it offensive. We shared our interpretations and had a good laugh.

The situation clearly demonstrated that things only mean what we determine their meaning to be. All things are filtered through our own interpretations. We may be well served to occasionally reexamine the meanings we apply, the interpretations we make.

There is no better area for such reevaluation than the issue of weight loss. If you have decided in your mind that you are committed to trying this program because you believe the research and have faith in the results you can achieve, BUT you believe that it will make you totally miserable, then you will set yourself up to fail! Why? Because you will do more to pass up the pain (experienced by following the eating program that you believe will make you TOTALLY miserable) than you will to pursue the pleasure of getting back into those jeans that have been hanging in the back of your closet!

How Do You Ensure a Psychology of Success?

You can ensure your own success by addressing several areas of your own psychology. The first is to set yourself up to succeed in light of the dance with pain and pleasure.

Here is how I suggest you do that.

Write your goal weight here: _____
Write your goal size here: _____

Describe your goal energy level here:

_____

_____

_____

Describe your goal health here:

_____

_____

_____

Take a moment to close your eyes and visualize yourself at this weight, this size, this energy level, and in this kind of excellent health. Get a picture of yourself. See yourself looking great, feeling great. Get a glimpse of your eyes. What do you see there? Keep that picture before you. Imagine it posted on the back of your eyelids so that you can see it each time you close your eyes.

Now, when you achieve that level of health and fitness, what benefits will it bring into your life? How will you feel about yourself? How will it affect your relationships? What positive impact will it have? (Examples: I will feel more like playing with my children when I get home from work; I will live to see my grandchildren born, etc.)

_____

_____

_____

_____

_____

_____

_____

_____

_____

_____

_____

_____

If you do not achieve that level of health and fitness, if you stay as you are now, or even get worse, what will that choice cost you? How will you feel about yourself? How will that choice affect your relationships? What impact will it have on your life? (Example: My child will be raised by another woman; I will be too ashamed to go out in public; I will lose all confidence in myself; I may die early from heart disease like so many of the men in my family have, etc.)

_____

_____

_____

_____

_____

_____

_____

_____

_____

Are these the results you want? Is that outcome what you deserve? Of course not! But you must keep the costs in front of you in order to keep yourself on track. Knowing the benefits (pleasure) of a healthy eating plan is important, but that knowledge will never create the motivation delivered by "passing up the pain" of failing to achieve it!

Your Interpretation of the Plan

You must choose to interpret this plan in a way that supports your success if it is to work for you. If you choose to label it as "the worst thing I've ever had to do" you're setting yourself up for failure.

Here is my suggestion: I highly recommend that you decide you can abide by this plan and enjoy it for 10 days. Resolve to reevaluate your interpretation after 10 days. My hunch is that you will feel so much better that you'll have no difficulty giving it a lifetime "thumbs up."

Remember, this program is not about counting, weighing, measuring, or starving. It's about eliminating a few things, rearranging the times of day you eat some things, and feeling better with each new day!

You can do it!

Write your positive, exciting interpretation of the program here:

_____

_____

_____

_____

Asking Yourself: "What Is This About?"

Another part of your psychology that must be addressed is the reason you reach for snacks. (There is always a reason—no exceptions.) We become so accustomed to grabbing snacks that we think doing so is simply a habit. But underneath, there is a reason.

There is no mystical formula for determining the reason. It's quite simple. Each time you find yourself reaching for a snack, pause and ask yourself, "what is this about?" You will be amazed what you learn.

In my clinical practice, I teach this exercise regularly. What I learn from those who practice asking themselves this question is interesting and often entertaining. I ask patients to keep a record and bring it into their sessions so that we can review it and find alternatives. I have heard and read many "reasons" that come from the asking. I have listed some of them below, along with the alternatives we chose.

REASON: "I learned that when I reach for a snack in the middle of the afternoon, I am really wanting to get rid of the bad breath I feel like I have from lunch. So I eat something to cover it up."

ALTERNATIVE: Using mouthwash or brushing your teeth.

REASON: "I am nervous, and food calms me down."

ALTERNATIVE: Taking in a deep breath to the count of 5, holding it to the count of 10, and letting it out to the count of 15. Repeat that sequence five times.

REASON: "I found out that when I'm lonely, I reach for food."

ALTERNATIVE: Call a friend or a mentor (you will read more about mentors later).

REASON: "I realized that I use it to nurture myself and take myself back to the nurturing of my mother. She always had cookies ready for me when I came home from school."

ALTERNATIVES: Nurture yourself by looking through a photo album containing pictures of your mom, by taking a bubble bath, by propping your feet up, or by asking for nurturing from a loved one.

REASON: "I find myself eating a snack just because it's around. It's like it's in my mouth before I even realize I am eating it."

ALTERNATIVE: Set your environment up for success. Remove all foods that are just "hanging around" waiting to be eaten.

Many of us go through life on auto-pilot. We never take the time to ask ourselves, "What is this about?" We either never pause to consider, or we assume there is some deep-seated psychological reason for our behavior.

Rarely is hunger the reason for snacking.

In her books *Fat is a Family Affair* and *Fat and Furious,* Judy Hollis offers a fascinating perspective on what thoughtless eating is about.

> You are fat and furious, but it's not about food. It's about your life. You find yourself addicted, depressed, and insatiable. But what you're really hungering for is to know your true self, to live an authentic life, to make your life count! The problem is, you don't know how to begin. That's why you're fat and furious. (Hollis, 1994)

In many ways, I think this author's statements are very true! We are hungering for an authentic life, a life that counts. For this same reason, I created a company, Let's Celebrate!, Inc., that offers this book in a seminar form.

Let's Celebrate! also offers many other seminars about living a life beyond extraordinary. People from all over the nation train to do these seminars. These individuals are motivated to help others; they want a life that counts, a life that leaves a legacy of mentorship. Perhaps deep down, that is what we are all hungering for!

Old Issues That Raise Their Heads

As a therapist, I have worked for years with adult survivors of childhood trauma, including physical abuse, sexual abuse, mental and emotional abuse, loss of parents or siblings, physical disabilities, and accidents. When these issues remain unaddressed, they have an impact on eating patterns and ultimately on weight.

These issues may be addressed in a variety of ways. You can seek counseling, find a support group, attend classes or seminars. I worked for years with these issues in several practice venues, and I realized that many people could not afford therapeutic intervention.

I spent a number of years establishing support groups to address various topics. I now teach seminars to assist people in working through old issues in an expedient manner.

Get whatever help you need. But don't use your old issues as an excuse. Don't wear them as a badge and blame your physical condition on your past. Take charge. Make this declaration: "The past is past! At last, at last!" I have people repeat that statement with me in many seminars.

Recently I was teaching a financial seminar and worked with a great young man who was bound up in old issues that were affecting his financial success (or lack of it!). I had him make the declaration and then told him to take a lap around the room. He started around the room slowly at first, declaring: "The past is past! At last, at last!" Everyone cheered and applauded him (and vicariously let go of some of their own old financial issues). As they did, his pace picked up and his declaration became more firm. "The past is past! At last, at last!"

You do the same. Take a lap around the block and declare to yourself: "The past is past! At last, at last!" It's a brand new day. You are in charge of your life. Don't let your past be in charge of your life!

By the way, you may be thinking, "Well, I read it and thought it and that's enough for me."

Don't make that mistake. We have learned through years of research that all major life changes occur when you DO SOMETHING that involves your body, your mind, your spirit, all engaging in something different and sometimes outrageous.

We all think about making changes and then are a bit surprised when nothing actually happens. If you want to achieve something you've never achieved, you must do something you've never done!

Now, get up and take a lap around your desk, around your sofa, or around your car, and declare: "The past is past! At last, at last!" Do it with feeling. Mean it!

Make a Resolution

You must *resolve* to follow this plan if you are to be successful. "Trying" means I will do it until I experience any discomfort or difficulty; then I will quit. Trying isn't enough. You must resolve to do it! RESOLVE!

What does resolve mean? It means to declare a firm decision with conviction.

Try this with me. Sit in a slumped position with your arms crossed and resting on your stomach and say in a wimpy tone of voice: "I guess I'll try this program." How does that feel? Does it feel like success? Does it elicit determination and courage? Of course not!

Now try this. Stand up. Stand tall and proud. Stand as you would stand if you were on the podium receiving your gold medal at the Olympics and they were playing your national anthem. Standing in that posture, declare: "I am taking charge of my weight, my health, and my destiny!" Do it again. Declare it with conviction.

Remember, you can't just read these words passively and expect an incredible result. When I ask people to do these exercises in my seminars, and I explain the significance of doing it with "gusto," I can look out over the audience and predict who will be successful.

Several months ago, a quiet young woman was in the crowd. She had been withdrawn and sullen through much of the meeting. When I explained that you must do something you've never done with great resolve to get your old ways of doing things dislodged, I saw her become totally involved in the exercise. She was jumping and swinging her arms and declaring her success at the top of her lungs.

Last evening, she came to give her testimonial at another seminar. In 10 weeks, she has gone from a dress size 24 to size 16 jeans! And she has only just begun!

That is the kind of resolution that is required for your success.

I am aware that more than half of you have read through the above paragraphs with amusement and never said a word out loud or got out of your seat. If you want to stay the way you've been, keep doing what you've always done. If you want to find new success, try something new. I believe if you truly want success, you must begin by stepping out of your comfort zone.

Now, once again. Stand up. Stand tall and proud. Stand as you would stand if you were on the podium receiving your gold medal at the Olympics, and they were playing your national anthem. Standing in that posture, declare: "I am taking charge of my weight, my health, and my destiny!" Do it again. Declare it with conviction.

I predict that those who are courageous enough to do this little exercise, right there in your home, or your office, or wherever you happen to be, those are the people who will be successful! My hat is off to you, my heart is open to you, and my hands are clapping for you!

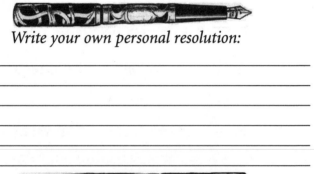

Write your own personal resolution:

_____

_____

_____

_____

_____

Now stand tall and proud and make your declaration with courage and conviction!

Old Beliefs That Don't Support You

Many of us have old beliefs that don't support us, beliefs that are detrimental to our success. We are not even aware we hold these beliefs, and yet they undermine any possibility of achieving our goals and our dreams.

I want to assist you in recognizing what they are, and then in CHANGING them.

Get a pen or pencil and write the answers to these questions or complete these sentences.

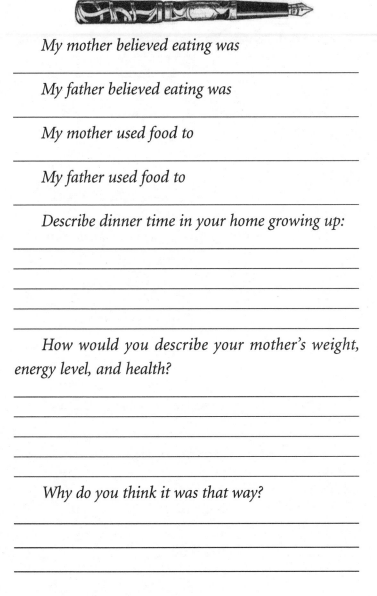

My mother believed eating was

_____

My father believed eating was

_____

My mother used food to

_____

My father used food to

_____

Describe dinner time in your home growing up:

_____

_____

_____

_____

How would you describe your mother's weight, energy level, and health?

_____

_____

_____

_____

Why do you think it was that way?

_____

_____

_____

How would you describe your father's weight, energy level, and health?

_____
_____
_____
_____
_____

Why do you think it was that way?

_____
_____
_____
_____
_____

When a challenge arose, how did your mother handle it?

_____
_____
_____
_____
_____

When a challenge arose, how did your father handle it?

_____
_____
_____
_____

I believe eating is

_____

I use food to

_____

Describe dinner time in your home now:

_____

_____

_____

_____

_____

How would you describe your weight, energy level, and health?

_____

_____

_____

_____

_____

Why do you think it is that way?

_____

_____

_____

_____

_____

When a challenge arises, how do you handle it?

_____

_____

_____

_____

What do you believe about a plan working for you?

_____

_____

_____

_____

_____

What do you believe about this plan working for you?

_____

_____

_____

_____

_____

What do you believe about having time to follow this plan?

_____

_____

_____

_____

_____

What do you believe about you being important enough to take the time and special considerations to follow this plan?

_____

_____

_____

_____

What do you believe about your ability to succeed at this plan or your ability to succeed in general?

_____

_____

_____

_____

Why on earth did I have you write the answers to these questions? In the answers to these questions, I would be willing to bet that you found some of your beliefs. Some of our beliefs are installed early in life as a result of our experience growing up. Some of them were helpful then but are not helpful now. Some of them were not helpful then and still aren't!

Which of these beliefs will NOT support your success? Write them below:

_____

_____

_____

_____

_____

_____

_____

I would be willing to bet some of your old beliefs that do not support you might be reflections of this fact: Of every 200 people who start a diet, 190 of them fail. Not only do they fail to lose their weight, but they begin gaining it back before they ever reach their goal weight (Schwartz, 1990).

You've heard these kinds of things again and again…and you have said, "I know that's right!" Does that belief support your success?

NO!

Has it ever crossed your mind to make a resolution (a firm decision with conviction) that you WILL BECOME one of the 10 who succeed?

That's what you must do. Examine your former beliefs and GET RID OF THE ONES THAT DON'T WORK! If you keep believing what you have always believed, you will keep getting the results you've always had! It's time for new and different results, right?

Therefore, you must adopt a new set of beliefs. For every old belief written above, convert it to a new belief that supports your success. For example, instead of "I guess I'll always struggle with my weight because everyone in my family has," try "I am determined to succeed because it will set an example that could change the health of my entire family!"

Instead of "I guess I'm just doomed to be depressed and tired," try "It's NEVER too late and I CAN and WILL take charge of my destiny!"

Use vocabulary that is zippy! Use phrases that will zap you when you need encouragement! Instead of "I will do this so I can look better," try "I am unstoppable: I'm going to look and feel like a million bucks!" Instead of "I don't have time to eat right," try "Just think of all the extra time I'll have when I don't have to fall on the sofa in exhaustion every evening at 7:45! YAHOO!"

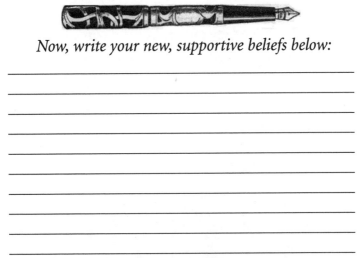

Now, write your new, supportive beliefs below:

_____
_____
_____
_____
_____
_____
_____
_____
_____

Now, one more step: Stand up and proclaim each of your new beliefs out loud. Use your body. Gesture as if you were a politician attempting to win a crowd. (You do have a crowd to win, those old voices within that you've listened to far too long!) Shout as if you were an evangelist with a burning message. (You do have a burning message and YOU are the one who needs to hear it!) Dance as if no one were watching— and if they are, just close the blinds!

You can succeed. You can have the body, the energy, the health, the radiant life you desire. But you MUST DETERMINE to achieve it. It will not come and knock on your front door.

And even if a new radiant life did come knocking on your door, you shouldn't be in there waiting. You need to be out taking a walk, going for a run, riding your bike, or skating, because...[read on]

Chapter 8

Exercise Is Not a Four-letter Word

If you exercise above your target heart range, your body dumps insulin.

I know many of you hoped that exercise would not appear as a topic in this book. I find a certain dread to be a fairly normal reaction. However, if you want optimum health, you MUST include exercise! Of course, you should consult your physician before beginning a new exercise program or making a change in your current regimen.

At one time in the history of America, an exercise program was unnecessary. After all, you would begin your day going out to the barn. You would milk your cows (using those quads to stoop), then carry heavy buckets of milk back to the house (using those pecs, biceps, and triceps). You would churn your butter (using those lats). Add to that carrying firewood in, hoeing and weeding your garden, harvesting your produce and carrying heavy buckets of vegetables, etc. No wonder exercise programs were unnecessary.

Now we find the exertion inconvenient if the batteries in the remote control fail and we must struggle up from our recliners to change the television channel! We fight for the closest parking place at the mall; we order groceries online to be delivered at our front door; we have intercoms so that we can speak to our children upstairs without having to climb the stairs.

We begin to see why we MUST incorporate an exercise program into our lives, and I'm going to give you several basic guidelines for doing so:

1) Always exercise with a heart monitor.
2) Get at least 20 minutes of aerobic/cardiovascular workout five times each week.
3) Select exercise that you enjoy.
4) Incorporate at least two strength-training exercises weekly.

Heart Monitor

Why do I recommend exercising with a heart monitor? First, the highest purpose for exercise in our program is the quality of your cardiovascular health, and this objective is more important than weight loss, fat loss, and increased energy (although these purposes are served as well). If you are not exercising in the appropriate range, you are simply burning calories.

Second, glucagon is only released when you exercise within your target heart range. If you exercise above your target heart range, your body dumps insulin. Do you ever find it perplexing when professional athletes die of heart problems? The explanation could be in the research cited earlier: Insulin levels are the single greatest predictor of heart attack risk. Some professional athletes train continuously with their heart rate above their target heart range.

It is crucial to exercise within your target heart range.

Third, when you exercise within the recommended guidelines for your age, you also continue to burn calories at twice the normal rate for several hours, an excellent argument for working out before eating.

How do you identify your ideal aerobic/cardiovascular workout range? The materials that accompany your heart monitor will contain all of the specific information. You can also go to this website which quickly calculates the range in which you get your ideal workout: http://www.healthatoz.com/atoz/fitness/tools/thr/one.asp.

Basically, the formula for figuring your heart rate is as follows:

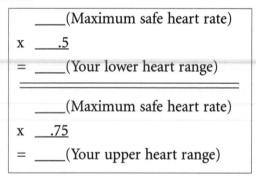

	220
—	____ (Your age)
=	____ (Maximum safe heart rate)

You should exercise between 50 and 75 percent of that rate.

	____ (Maximum safe heart rate)
x	.5
=	____ (Your lower heart range)
	____ (Maximum safe heart rate)
x	.75
=	____ (Your upper heart range)

You want to make sure that your heart rate remains between these two levels as you work out. If you exercise above your upper heart range, you could strain your heart. If you exercise below your lower heart range, you are simply burning a few extra calories.

People who are unaccustomed to exercise are often surprised by what they learn when they first use a heart monitor. Sometimes we perceive a level of exertion very differently from its actual load on our heart muscle. **Remember that the point of exercise is not how fast your feet are moving; the point is how fast your heart is pumping.**

Until you purchase your heart monitor, you may check your heart rate by placing your index and middle fingers on your neck or your wrist and finding your pulse. You may take it for 10 seconds and multiply the number of beats by 6, or take it for 6 seconds and multiply the number of beats by 10, to find your current heart rate.

You should only use this manual method for a short time until you have the opportunity to purchase your heart monitor. It's difficult to concentrate on exertion and the heart monitoring simultaneously, and it's easy to forget to continually monitor your pulse. In the heat of the moment, a beginner can readily forget himself and exceed the upper safe limit of exertion.

Where can you purchase a heart monitor? Most sporting goods stores carry the units, and retailers who specialize in running gear generally offer several models. Quite often you can get an excellent price by shopping online. The following website provides a good description of the various brands and their functions: http://www.heart-rate-monitor.net.

My personal favorite at this time is the LifeSource XC300. This model has all of the necessary functions, and the user can replace the batteries (a useful and unusual feature). Some heart monitors must be sent to the manufacturer for battery replacement, and this process can take from three to six weeks.

The 20 – 5 Formula

As an absolute bare minimum, your heart needs a 20-minute aerobic workout five times a week! Research has shown that our heart has received its minimum workout needed for optimal functioning following a 20-minute workout. Why 20 minutes? It takes 12 minutes for your metabolism to enter the fat-burning zone (Bailey, 1978) and it would be a shame to arrive at the zone and not spend some time there, burning fat!

Kenneth Cooper was one of the first physicians to begin the crusade for taking care of our hearts through aerobic exercise. He said,

> Longevity does not depend on the strength and tone of the muscles of the arms, legs, or abdominal wall. According to our present understanding of the matter, it is much more likely, in the absence of organic disease elsewhere, to depend on the capability of the cardiovascular and pulmonary systems to withstand the stresses of modern living. (Cooper, 1980)

Why aerobic exercise instead of just playing golf or tennis? Because ONLY aerobic workouts release glucagon, the magic bullet that ushers fat out of your fat cells (Waterhouse, 1993).

There is no research indicating that a particular time of day is best for exercise. I recommend that you schedule it, just as you schedule other important meetings in your life. Get up 20 minutes earlier in the morning; schedule exercise during your lunch break; take 20 minutes in the evening when you get home.

I find that when people start with a 20-minute commitment, they are soon willing to expand the time when possible. If I suggest a 45-minute workout, however, the response I most often hear is: "I just don't have that kind of time." Begin with a commitment for 20 minutes of exercise at least five times each week and see what happens!

Select an Exercise That You Enjoy

It is very important that you find an exercise that you can enjoy. I remember when a colleague in graduate school asked me if I would coach her in her weight loss program. I agreed, and we established her plan that included 20 minutes of aerobic workout daily, Tuesday through Saturday.

It became apparent that the exercise was the most difficult part of the program for her. I asked her what she was doing for her exercise. With great disdain, she moaned, "the stupid treadmill." I knew immediately that the "stupid treadmill" would never work for her.

I asked her why she was using the treadmill and her response was, "because it's in the bedroom." I asked her if she would take a seat in an electric chair just because it happened to be in her bedroom. We both laughed, and she got the point.

She arranged to have the Salvation Army pick up the treadmill, and we explored activities she really enjoyed. I learned that she had been a "disco queen" in her earlier years. We went together to a used music store and found her old disco favorites. She began to spend 20, then 30, then 45 minutes daily dancing up a storm to all of her old favorite tunes.

Be creative! Go on bike rides with your kids; go on walks with your friends; find a Jazzercise class; get an aqua jogger and jog in the swimming pool. (You can read about and order an aqua jogger online at www.bodytrends.com/aqua.htm.)

Incorporate at Least Two Strength-training Workouts Weekly

There are numerous reasons why strength-training workouts should be part of your lifestyle. Resistance training

* increases your metabolic rate,
* develops and restores bone density,
* increases lean muscle mass,
* increases endurance,
* improves balance,
* decreases risk of coronary disease, and
* provides vibrancy.

When you incorporate a strength-training workout with your aerobic workout, you increase the accelerated calorie burning for up to 15 hours (*Burn Fat Faster*, 1998).

Three times weekly, I combine an aerobic workout with strength training. I begin with 15 minutes on the elliptical trainer, then do one set of upper body exercises, one set of lower body strength-training drills.

My goal is toning, so I do 15 rapid repetitions per set. If your goal is building mass, choose greater weights and do 10 to 12 slow repetitions.

I then return to another piece of cardiovascular training equipment (treadmill, stair stepper, climber, cross country skier, bike) or run around the track. Then I go for the next set.

A regimen like this one is easier to do if you have either a small gym at home or a membership at a health club. I highly recommend memberships at your local YMCA. The facilities are generally well equipped, and the rates are affordable. Various books and resources are available to show how to use things around your house for workouts. You can purchase weights and workout instructions at www.leiweights.com.

Following an accident in which I broke my leg in four places and had a replacement for my ACL (Anterior Cruciate Ligament—the ligament in the knee that connects the upper and lower leg bones, stabilizing knee movements), I had to strengthen my quads. Since I was still not weight-bearing, it was difficult to get around the gym on crutches. Instead, I got a plastic grocery bag and put two cans of green beans in it. I sat on my kitchen table, hung the bag on my foot at my ankle and raised and lowered it 15 times per set. As my strength increased, I added another can of green beans.

The most effective means of exercise, the way to get the "most bang for your buck," is to incorporate an aerobic/cardiovascular exercise with a strength-training workout. Some people refer to this approach as the "circuit" or "super circuit." Some gyms are designed for this approach with weight training equipment around a running track.

I recently received an email from a friend at my church who knows that I am an exercise fanatic. It was a "secret about building tremendous arm muscles." Here is a summary of that email:

You begin with a 5-pound potato sack in each arm and hold them outstretched as long as possible (until your arms begin to tremble). When you've mastered that, you graduate to 10-pound potato sacks. Then finally, as your strength increases, you move up to 20-pound potato sacks.

It costs you practically nothing, you don't have to get in your car and go to a gym, and you can do it any time of the day or night. THEN, after you've mastered the 20-pound potato sack, you begin to place potatoes in the sack!

Chapter 9

Are There Any Shortcuts?

A rate of one to three
pounds weekly is the safest
recommended rate for
long-term success.

I am certain you will get results if you follow the program in this book. I am equally certain that some people will want to know if they can achieve them quicker!

You want to lose weight at a moderate rate. A rate of one to three pounds weekly is the safest recommended rate for long-term success. However, if you are not achieving those rates, here are a few hints that may accelerate your progress.

1) Here is one particular shortcut that works extremely well for most people. Eat the same menu daily for a week to 10 days. I first learned about it to my own amazement when I was in college. I

hardly had time to think about anything other than course work, and there was no time for preparing food. I fell into a rhythm of sorts, eating the same thing every day. I have never been much of a breakfast eater, so my first meal came during my break between my early morning and afternoon classes. I would go across the street from the classroom to the convenience store and get a large cherry-cola slushy and a large bag of barbecue-flavored corn chips. I would eat and drink these items in class. On my way to my practicum site (an hour's drive), I would pass through a fast-food restaurant and order the same thing: a fried chicken breast, a fried chicken drumstick, mashed potatoes and gravy, and a roll with honey butter. I would eat this on the drive. (Yes, I know how dangerous that is!) When I completed my practicum hours each evening, I would stop for a double dip of chocolate-mint ice cream. You may find this difficult to believe, but I lost more than 10 pounds the first month I ate this diet! However, when I changed the routine, I gained it all back. I now believe that the weight loss occurred because my body knew exactly how much insulin would be needed at what time of the day. Therefore, it did not make additional insulin dumps. I do not recommend the above diet in any shape, form, or fashion! But here is the shortcut I recommend. For a week to 10 days, decide on your diet and repeat it each day. I would recommend the following:

a) For breakfast – one of the high-protein casseroles found in the *Companion Guide*

b) For lunch – a grilled chicken Caesar salad (no croutons)

c) For dinner – a salad, a piece of fowl or fish, a high-protein veggie, and a whole-grain roll

If you must have a snack, eat the same high-protein snack daily.

2) If you are not achieving weight loss of one to three pounds each week, you might consider reducing or eliminating cheese. Although it is a high-protein food, it can prohibit weight loss in some people. If you can't seem to give up cheese altogether, consider some of the lower fat versions (low-fat or fat-free cheddar, Jarlsberg, etc.).

3) Drink more water. You hear it everywhere, and it's true! You need more water. Many times we think we're hungry when we're really thirsty. In his book, *Your Body's Many Cries for Water*,

Batmanghelidj explains that not only can consuming more water assist in weight loss, but it is also the healing foundation of many other remedies. You may learn more about this concept on his website, www.watercure.com.

4) Do not combine this eating program with ANY OTHER eating plan! Many people mistakenly think that they can combine a bit of this program with a bit of that program. You CANNOT! Most programs have merit in and of themselves, but few work well when combined with other programs. Follow this program SPECIFICALLY!

5) Increase your exercise! If you are doing your 20-minute workout five times a week, either add time to your current routine or create exercise throughout the day. For example, take the parking spot farthest from your office. When you take the up or down escalator, walk even while it is in motion. Instead of sending an email to your coworker down the hall, take a walk to deliver the message. My mother does an excellent job of finding spontaneous opportunities for exercise. She lives upstairs and makes sure she goes up and down the stairs 10 to 12 times daily in addition to her regular walking routine.

6) Exercise for 10 to 15 minutes before you go to bed. If you would like your body to keep burning calories and fat while you sleep, slip in a 10- to 15-minute exercise session an hour before you tuck yourself in!

7) Eliminate all diet drinks other than those sweetened with Splenda™ (sucralose). Splenda™ is the only artificial sweetener that does not cause an insulin spike. You can visit their website for more information: www.splenda.com.

8) Reduce or eliminate stress. When we experience stress, our bodies dump insulin into our systems. Learn some stress management techniques. There are countless books, tapes, and seminars available on stress management. My favorite stress management technique, and one I teach in my classes, is as follows: Take a moment and think about what really matters in life. Get beyond the bills that are due, your "to do" list, and the argument you had with your spouse this morning. What really matters? Then write a gratitude list. What are you grateful for? When she was asked to identify the most impactful thing in her life, Oprah responded: "Keeping a gratitude journal."

9) Take a nutritional supplement designed to increase your energy level and assist in your weight and fat loss. There are many on the market. I highly recommend that you avoid those that contain mahuang, effedra or effedrine, and caffeine. I developed my own nutritional system after years of listening to the needs of my audiences. Early clinical trials (double-blind placebo) indicated weight loss, fat loss, increase in energy, increase in libido, better state of mind (less depression and anxiety), more restful sleep, and lowered cholesterol and blood pressure.

Chapter 10

Some Helpful Tips

Tracking your body fat is more important than tracking your weight.

As you begin your journey of success, here are some tips that may help you along your way.

1) Do NOT weigh daily! At most, weigh twice weekly, and I recommend that you weigh yourself only once each week. Your body weight can fluctuate drastically according to your water intake and release. Most people become easily discouraged if the scales reflect an increase. You should weigh once weekly on the same day, at the same time, preferably without clothing so that you do not have to average the weight of your clothing and shoes.

What's a Nice Person Like Me...

2) Obtain a scale that measures fat loss. Tanita has created an entire line of scales that can be easily programmed with your gender and height. When you step on the scales, built-in electrodes use a Bioelectrical Impedance Analysis (BIA) to 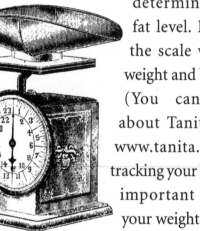 determine your body fat level. In five seconds the scale will flash your weight and body fat results. (You can read more about Tanita products at www.tanita.com.) In fact, tracking your body fat is more important than tracking your weight.

According to the American Council on Exercise, here are the recommended body fat percentages:

Classification	Women (% fat)	Men (% fat)
Essential Fats %s	10-12%	2-4%
Professional Athletes	14-20%	6-13%
Physically Fit	21-24%	14-17%
Average	25-31%	18-25%
Obese	32% plus	25% plus

I recently had a client who was following my program closely. The appearance of her face indicated weight loss, yet she was so very discouraged that she hadn't lost a pound. I encouraged her to obtain a fat measuring scale, but before she ever purchased one, she came in announcing that she had dropped one jeans size. Although she saw no weight loss, fat loss was obviously occurring.

3) Discard your "fat clothes" as you lose weight. When you tuck them into the back of your closet, you are p s y c h o l o g i c a l l y preparing yourself to use them again. Determine that you will not go back to that size, and take them to a women's shelter, Goodwill, Salvation Army, or other charitable organization.

4) While you are dropping off your outsized clothes with a charitable organization, shop for some clothing for your new size. If you are now at your goal weight, you will still want some new clothes to

show off your new body. When I suggest this, I quite often see a shocked expression and a snarl: "I wouldn't be caught dead buying my clothes there." Why not? Many of the clothes you delivered were excellent clothes of high quality. Others have brought theirs in for similar reasons. I have a good friend who is a first-class lady. She shops in thrift stores regularly, although you would never believe it. She shows up for every event "dressed to the nines." Yet the reason she has so many fabulous clothes is that she goes on "treasure hunts." Indeed she finds them!

5) Keep prepared foods on hand. When I make the casseroles and dishes you will find in the *Companion Guide,* I make them in large quantities and freeze them in single-serving quantities in

GladWare®. After just five minutes in the microwave, they are ready! One of the reasons many people resort to poor food choices is that fast food is just that—quickly available. If you keep your own prepared foods at all times, there is no reason to fall back on junk or fast food. In addition, you can buy large bags of prepared chicken breasts, meatballs, steaks, etc. at Sam's Club warehouse, Costco, or large groceries. Keeping these supplies in the freezer for a quick snack or meal is also very convenient!

6) FIND A MENTOR! The theme of my company, Let's Celebrate!, Inc., is mentorship. A mentor is a trusted guide, someone who has success or experience in the area of weight loss, energy revitalization, or excellent health, someone who believes in you, who will cheer you on, and who will gently nudge you back onto your path when you become sidetracked. A mentor will do EVERYTHING possible to help ensure your success.

7) BECOME A MENTOR! As you achieve success, offer to mentor someone else you know to be struggling with similar issues. Such people will not be difficult to find! As you coach someone else to succeed, you will become further committed to your own personal

What's a Nice Person Like Me....

success. Just think what a difference it could make if we all had a bit of success and coached someone else in that direction. The obesity rates in the United States could drop significantly if we all did our small part. That is the vision of my company, Let's Celebrate!...

TO CHANGE THE WORLD...ONE HEART AT A TIME!

Bibliography

AHA (American Heart Association). "High Blood Levels of Insulin Possible Independent Predictor of Heart Attack Risk." *American Heart Association Journal.* NR 98-4927, 1998.

Applegate, L. "Protein Confusion." *WebMd.* http://my.webmd.com/content/article/1671.51572, 2001.

Appleton, N. "Sugar 'N Spice and Everything Nice." *Healthy Child Online.* http://www.healthychild.com/database/sugar_n_spice_and_everything_nice.htm, 2002.

Bailey, C. *Fit or Fat.* Boston: Houghton Mifflin Co., 1978.

Batmanghelidj, F. *Your Body's Many Cries for Water.* Falls Church, Virginia: Global Health Solutions, 1980.

"Burn Fat Faster." *Father's World.* http://www.fathersworld.com, 1998.

Bohorquez, E. "The In's and Out's of Licking Sugar Addiction." http://www.sugar-addiction.com. Sarasota Medical Hypnosis Institute, 2001.

CNN.com. "New Research Supports Health Benefits of Red Wine." http://www.cnn.com/2000/HEALTH/diet.fitness/07/03/french.paradox/, July 3, 2000.

Cooper, K. *Aerobics.* New York: Bantam Books, 1980.

Diamond, M. and D. Schnell. *Fitonics for Life*. New York: Avon Books, 1996.

Duffy, W. *Sugar Blues*. New York: Warner Books, 1975.

Eades, M.R. and M.D. Eades. *Protein Power*. New York: Bantam Books, 1996.

Fontbonne, A., M.A. Charles, N. Thibult, J.L. Richard, J.R. Claude, J.M. Warnet, G.E. Rosseline, and E. Eschwege. "Hyperinsulinemia as a Predictor of Coronary Heart Disease Mortality in Healthy Population: The Paris Prospective Study, 1-Year Follow-Up." *Diabetologia*. Volume 34, Number 5, 1991, 356-361.

Fuh, M., D.A. Shieh, Y.D. Wu, I. Chen, and G.M. Reaven. "Abnormalities of Carbohydrate and Lipid Metabolism in Patients with Hypertension." *Archives of Internal Medicine*. Volume 147, June 1987, 1035-1038.

Gittleman, A.L. *Get the Sugar Out*. New York: Three Rivers Press, 1996.

Goldman, J., et al. "Behavioral Effects of Sucrose on Preschool Children." *Journal of Abnormal Child Psychology*. Volume 14, Number 4, 1986, 565-577.

Gwinup, G. and A.N. Elias. "Hypothesis: Insulin Is Responsible for the Vascular Complications of Diabetes." *Medical Hypotheses*. Volume 34, Number 1, 1991, 689-693.

Haffner, S.M. "Epidemiology of Insulin Resistance and Its Relation to Coronary Artery Disease." *American Journal of Cardiology*. Volume 84, Number 1, July 8, 1999, 11-14.

Heller, R., and R. Heller. *The Carbohydrate Addict's LifeSpan Program*. New York: Penguin Group, 1998.

Heller, R., R. Heller, and F. Vagnini. *The Carbohydrate Addict's Healthy Heart Program*. New York: Ballantine Books, 1999.

Hollis, J. *Fat and Furious*. New York: Ballantine Books, 1994.

Hollis, J. *Fat is a Family Affair*. Hazelden Information Education, 1996.

Ikeda, J.P. "Health Promotion: A Size Acceptance Approach." *Healthy Weight Journal*. Volume 14, Number 1, January/February 2000, 12.

Kennedy, R. "Addiction to Sugar." *The Doctor's Medical Library*. http://www.medical-library.net/sites/sugar_addiction.html, 2002.

Kennedy, R. "Yeast Syndrome." *The Doctor's Medical Library.* http://www.medical-library.net/sites/framer.html?/sites/_yeast_syndrome.html, 1999.

Lorenc, V. *La Vie Claire.* 1972.

Moore, N. *Designing Your Life with Designer Foods: The Facts about Phytochemicals.* Dallas, Texas: Charis Publishing, 1996.

NIH Technol Assess Statement Online. "Methods for Voluntary Weight Loss and Control." http://hstat.nlm.nih.gov/hq/Hquest/db/local.nih.taw.ta91.ta10/screen/DocTitle/s/35222, March 30, 1992.

Pyorala, M., H. Miettinen, M. Laakso, and K. Pyorala. "Hyperinsulinemia Predicts Coronary Heart Disease Risk in Healthy Middle-Aged Men: The 11-Year Follow-Up Results of the Helsinki Policemen Study." *Circulation.* Volume 98, Number 4, August 4, 1998, 398-404.

Reaven, G.M. "Role of Insulin Resistance in Human Disease: A Short History." *J Basic Clin Physiol Pharmacol.* Volume 9, 1991, 387-406.

Schlienger, J.L. "Alcohol and Cardiovacular System: Mechanisms of the Protective Effects." *Pathol Biol.* Volume 49, Number 9, November 2001, 764-768.

Schwartz, B. *Diets Still Don't Work!* Houston, Texas: Breakthrough Publishing, 1990.

Waterhouse, D. *Outsmarting the Female Fat Cell.* New York: Warner Books, 1993.

**For More Information
On Dr. Neecie Moore's Nutritional
Products and Seminars,
Contact:
Let's Celebrate!, Inc.
6100 Avenue K, Suite 110
Plano, TX 75074
Toll Free Order Line: 888-499-9888
214-289-7777
Fax: 972-881-8689
www.letscelebrate.com**

Index

Symbols

V

W

PROFICIENT

3

Simple Truths

and

6

Essential Traits

of

Powerful Writing

PRESTWICK HOUSE, INC.

"Everything for the English Classroom!"

Simple Truths
and

Essential Traits
of

Powerful Writing

SENIOR EDITOR: Douglas E. Grudzina

EDITOR: Mary C. Beardsley

BOOK DESIGN: Larry Knox

PRODUCTION: Jerry Clark

PRESTWICK HOUSE, INC.

P.O. Box 658 • Clayton, Delaware 19938

Tel: 1.800.932.4593

Fax: 1.888.718.9333

Web: www.prestwickhouse.com

ISBN 978-1-58049-323-9

Table of Contents

Continued on next page

PROFICIENT

3
Simple Truths
and

6
Essential Traits
of

Powerful Writing

PRESTWICK HOUSE, INC.
"Everything for the English Classroom!"

Essential Traits

OVER THE PAST SEVERAL YEARS, two trends in writing instruction have grown in popularity: primary trait instruction and trait-based scoring. Both of these trends carry great benefits for the students, but their effectiveness is limited by how they are understood and implemented in today's classrooms. The Prestwick House *Simple Truths* series hopes to overcome a few of these limitations.

Primary Trait Instruction comes packaged under a number of names, and is probably the most popular method of teaching writing. It is based on the premise that there are six (some editors opt for five traits while others promote seven traits; we feel six cover writing instruction best) essential characteristics or "traits" to a piece of writing and that each of these traits can be taught separately. These traits can then be combined at some point to produce a good essay.

Throughout the *Simple Truths* series, we will focus on the traits of **Development and Elaboration, Organization, Sentence Structure and Variety, Conventions of Written English, Word Choice,** and **Voice**. Each of these is explained in its own chapter.

Underlying the Six Essential Traits, however, are three simple principles, or truths, that *explain the need* for each of the traits in powerful writing.

A Review of the Three Truths:

By now you are familiar with the six essential traits of powerful writing: Development and Elaboration, Organization, Sentence Structure and Variety, Conventions of Written English, Word Choice, and Voice. Knowledge of these traits alone, however, will not give your writing the power you want. In order to write essays and papers that really stand out, you need to follow three Simple Truths of powerful writing.

| 1st Truth | Powerful writing really says something. |

ESSENTIAL TRAIT:

❶ Development and Elaboration

> Your writing needs a point and must contain important information you want to share with someone else.

| 2nd Truth | Powerful writing is understandable to others. |

ESSENTIAL TRAITS:

❷ Organization

❸ Sentence Structure and Variety

❹ Conventions of Written English

> You are writing to communicate your main idea with another person or other people. You will not be with the reader to explain what you mean, so what you write must be clear and understandable to your reader.

| 3rd Truth | Powerful writing is painless to read. |

ESSENTIAL TRAITS:

❺ Word Choice

❻ Voice

> Right now, you are writing largely to compete with other students for a high test score, placement in college, and possibly even scholarship money. Your essay should stand out and be a memorable, beneficial, and pleasant experience for your reader. Your writing should represent you as intelligent, organized, and thoughtful. You want your reader to have a positive feeling about you based on his or her experience reading your writing.

Applying
the
First Truth

3
Simple Truths
and

6
Essential Traits
of

Powerful Writing

DEVELOPMENT AND ELABORATION

Trait
One

> *Decide what corner of your subject you're going to bite off,*
> *and be content to cover it well and stop.*
> —William Zinsser, *On Writing Well*

Identifying a Powerful Research Topic

MANY COURSES and programs of study require end-of-course research projects. Whether the final product takes the form of an extended essay or formal research paper, an oral report or multimedia presentation, or something else, the keys to success are selecting the best topic and identifying the central purpose that will make your final presentation the strongest.

How many pages would it take you to write a paper on holidays in America? Think about it: what holidays will you cover? What aspects of the holidays will you discuss? The reason or purpose of the holiday? Its history? Associated traditions? Does "America" include just the United States or Canada and Mexico as well? How about Central and South America? By the time you add up all the information your holidays in America topic is going to need, you've committed yourself to years of research and a shelf of books!

As William Zinsser suggests, "decide what *corner of your subject* you're going to bite off." "Holidays in America" might become "the history of holidays in the United States," which is still broad. Thus, it might become "the history of Christmas in the United States," but you still have more than 200 years of history, as well as countless denominational and national contributions to the day's history. A much more reasonable "corner" to "bite off" would be something like "English and German roots of the United States' most popular Christmas traditions." While this topic still includes a good deal of information, it also excludes a lot and gives you a pretty specific guide to develop a thesis and outline to begin your search for information.

Make Yours Better!

Thesis is introduced clearly. We know what idea is going to be developed: the problem of a calendar that gradually got off track.

Although it may seem straightforward to calculate what day it is, there are actually many different ways to do it. One problem the Western calendar once had was that the months were based on the cycle of the moon (the word "month" actually comes from "moon"), while the year was based on the time it took the Earth to go around the sun. The cycles of the sun and moon do not match up, so the position of months in the year changed more and more as time went by, until eventually seasonal festivals that occurred in certain months were actually being celebrated in the wrong seasons.

The basic discrepancy between solar and lunar calendars is introduced.

Ancient cultures often used the lunar cycle to calculate their calendars. Each lunar month (the time from one full moon to the next) is about 29 and a half days long. Twelve of these periods add up to only 354 days. A solar year (the time from one vernal equinox to the next vernal equinox) is about 365 and a quarter days long. Every year, therefore, the vernal equinox was eleven days earlier than the year before. This meant that a certain festival supposed to be celebrated on a certain day of a particular month, for example a harvest festival on October 15, might not coincide with the seasonal event it was supposed to mark (October 15 would eventually fall during the summer) unless "extra" days were inserted into the calendar.

The October 15 harvest festival offers a concrete example of the potentially unclear concept of a seasonal holiday falling out of its season.

This paragraph shows us the results of the problem in a particular culture—that of ancient Rome. In fact, the problem seems to be solved here.

In ancient Rome, special priests, called pontifices, inserted an extra month (called an intercalary month) between two months every few years. During times of political strife, however, such as the periods during war, the calendar might be neglected, allowing the months to get out of sync with the solar year. In 45 B.C.E., Julius Caesar, following the science of the Greek astronomer Sosigenes, declared that the calendar would follow the seasons and be 365 and a quarter days long, with an "extra" day added every four years to compensate. This is why we know this calendar as the Julian calendar.

A little more information further develops the idea and lets the reader finish the passage feeling informed.

The Julian year was still a little off, however—eleven minutes longer every year. After a thousand years, the date of the vernal equinox was ten days earlier than it should have been. Pope Gregory XIII declared in 1582 that the vernal equinox would be on March 21 instead of March 11, the date it was scheduled to fall on that year.

He chose March 21 because that was the date of the equinox in 325 C.E., when the Council of Nicaea established the date of Easter as dependent upon the first full moon on or after the vernal equinox. With the equinox occurring earlier and earlier, Easter would eventually fall in the winter, and

Pope Gregory wanted to maintain the holy day as a spring festival. Catholic countries followed this change. The new calendar, called the Gregorian calendar, had a leap year every four years like the Julian calendar. However, there was also another rule to prevent the loss of days that had occurred with the Julian calendar: years that ended a century would be leap years only if they could be divided by four hundred. Thus, the years 1700, 1800, and 1900 were not "leap years," but the year 2000 was. This adjustment leads to the loss of only one day every 3000 years. The Gregorian calendar is the one followed by most Western countries today.

The calendar, whether printed or electronic, is as ubiquitous as the light bulb, and is an essential tool for society to plan its work, its vacations, and its holidays. Yet there is much, much more behind the cardboard chart printed with numbered boxes than most people realize.

■ Here again we have another concrete example to illustrate the difficult-to-understand point.

■ Mentioning the years 1799, 1800, and 1900 further provides concrete examples for a difficult concept.

Essay Critique

The author of this passage takes a main idea—the difference in calendar cycles—and develops it by giving specific information (the number of days in a lunar cycle, etc) about it. Then the author moves outward and shows how the Western world handled the problem, finally returning to the present day.

This essay receives a score of 10 on the:

Development and Elaboration Rubric

14 = ACCOMPLISHED
There are enough details, examples, anecdotes, supporting facts, etc., to give the reader a strong discussion. There is no needless information. Every word, phrase, clause, and sentence contributes to the main idea.

13 = The discussion is complete and sharply focused.

12 = The discussion is complete and focused.

11 = The discussion is complete and focused, but the reader is left with a sense that the topic has not really been exhausted.

10 = PROFICIENT
The main idea of the essay is clear. There is almost enough information for a full and complete discussion, but the reader is left with a few unanswered questions. The focus of the essay is clear, with a few lapses.

Narrowing Your Topic

Let's say you've just completed a course in twentieth-century American literature and are required to write a five-page (1,000 word) paper as a culminating assignment, a demonstration of your mastery of the course content.

Twentieth-century American literature is a huge field from which to draw a research topic. Narrow it down to "the twentieth-century American novel," and you still have a huge field. *What about* the twentieth-century American novel?

Narrow it down still further, and you might decide you want to write "something about" The Lost Generation. But what? You do not want to merely list the authors or their books. In academic writing, even in the end-of-course culminating project, your goal will essentially be to add your insight to the material you have studied. Therefore, you do not want merely to summarize the main events of their lives. You do not want merely to offer a definition of what The Lost Generation was. Neither of those would result in very interesting reports, and neither would really invite anything more than a repeat of exactly what you probably learned in class.

So you choose an author of the Lost Generation—F. Scott Fitzgerald. Now you need to think of what you want to *say* about him. Again, you do *not* want to offer a mere biography, a list of his titles, or summaries of his novels.

Now is when you apply the exercises you began to work on in the previous book.

When you think about, and perform some preliminary research on, the life and novels of F. Scott Fitzgerald and generally what the term "Lost Generation" refers to, you should begin to identify some potential approaches, a few interesting slants your report might take:

Example:
- *The Great Gatsby* as the *manifesto* of The Lost Generation
- The characters of Gatsby, Daisy, Nick, and Tom as *portraits* of Lost Generation values and behaviors
- How Fitzgerald's short stories illustrate the *social tension* and *shifting values* of post-World-War-I America

Here is where you need to think—not only in terms of the *subject matter*—but also in terms of *relationships*.

Exploring Relationships

Relationship:
   Sources of...
   Influences on...   }   **literary works or bodies of literature**
   Inspirations for...

Examples of Topics:
The Clutter family killings and Truman Capote's In Cold Blood *as America's first piece of "journalistic fiction"*
The impact of the Protestant Reformation on Renaissance literature

Relationship:
   Political
   Social   }   **contexts for literature and literary movements**
   Cultural

Examples of Topics:
Political, social, and economic background to the Romantic movement of the early nineteenth century
The role of the global corporation and consumerism in Aldous Huxley's Brave New World

Relationship:
   Impact of an event, invention or discovery on...

Examples of Topics:
Impact of Columbus' voyages on European theology and philosophy

Impact of the 9/11 attacks on...   { *... tourism in the United states*
   ... United States foreign policy in the twenty-first century

Impact of the internal combustion engine on...   { *... the family pollution*

Impact of the development of the World Wide Web on...   { *... personal communications*
   ... global economy and politics

Relationship:
    Causes of...
    Events leading to...
    Factors contributing to...

Examples of Topics:
Economic and political causes of the Great Depression
Biblical and theological roots of the current Middle East crises
Contributions of technological advances and social factors of the 1950s to the 1960s Women's Liberation movement

Exercise 1A: Brainstorming and Narrowing a Topic

For each subject below, list as many specific examples as you can.

1. Any title of fiction or nonfiction you read within the past two years:

2. Any historical period or event in which you are interested:

3. Any significant person (living or dead) and his or her accomplishments or "claim to fame":

4. Any current event or issue:

Exercise 1B: Brainstorming and Narrowing a Topic

Select specific examples from your above lists and use them to create narrowed-down topics for each of the relationships below.

1. Role of characters, conflicts, themes, literary devices [symbolism, imagery, etc.] in a work of literature or an author's body of work
   For example: Shakespeare's use of the supernatural to reflect the inner minds of his characters.

   Your Narrowed Topics:

2. Sources of, influences on, inspirations for literary works or bodies of literature
   For example: Historical and mythological sources for Shakespeare's most famous plays.

   Your Narrowed Topics:

3. Political, social, cultural contexts for literature and literary movements
   For example: The post-WW II atomic age and William Golding's Lord of the Flies.

   Your Narrowed Topics:

4. Impact of an event, invention or discovery on...
   For example: Impact of the discovery of the Dead Sea Scrolls on biblical scholarship.

   Your Narrowed Topics:

5. Causes of...; Events leading to...; Factors contributing to...

   Your Narrowed Topics:

You Still Need a Thesis

You know the four purposes for writing: to inform (expository writing), to persuade (persuasive or argumentative writing), to express personal opinions, feelings, reflections, etc. (personal writing), and to create literature ("creative" writing).

You also know the many modes of development that include narration, description, classification, comparison/contrast, process, cause and effect, and so on.

And in the previous book, you began to appreciate that *everything* you write needs to be centered on a thesis.

An *informative thesis* might be a mere introduction of a general (or little-known) fact:

- Few people realize that the printing press has its roots in the olive and grape presses used in the Mediterranean region since antiquity to produce oil and wine.

A *persuasive thesis* might actually invite disagreement:

- The printing press was not really as novel an idea as it is usually celebrated to be, but had its roots in technologies that had already been centuries old before Johann Gutenberg was even born.

A *personally expressive thesis* merely introduces a sentiment or opinion:

- The invention of the printing press is probably the most important event in Europe's transition from middle ages to Renaissance.

Exercise 2: Drafting a Thesis

Select one of the narrowed topics from each of the relationship sets in Exercise 1B and list the ones you've selected below:

1. Role of characters, conflicts, themes, literary devices [symbolism, imagery, etc.] in a work of literature or an author's body of work

2. Sources of, influences on, inspirations for literary works or bodies of literature

3. Political, social, cultural contexts for literature and literary movements

4. Impact of an event, invention or discovery on...

5. Causes of...; Events leading to...; Factors contributing to...

Informational: In one sentence, state a general or little-known fact about each topic.

For example:
Although the eruption of Mount Vesuvius that destroyed the city of Pompeii in the year 79 C.E. surprised tens of thousands of people and led to their deaths, the eruption did not occur without warning, and many lives could have been saved had those warnings been heeded.

1.

2.

3.

4.

5.

Expressive: In one sentence, state a point about each topic that you can demonstrate to be valid, but that invites disagreement and discussion.

For example:
The most important lesson to be learned from the massive loss of life during the destruction of Pompeii in the year 79 C.E. is that humans cannot afford to be complacent and overconfident in their "conquest" of nature.

(Notice that, even though this is a blatant statement of opinion, the writer does not need to write, "I feel," "I believe," or "in my opinion." To do so would not add any clarity to the statement and would actually weaken the writer's credibility.)

(Also note, however, that this thesis is a mere statement of opinion. It is not a call to action or a request for the reader to agree with it.)

1.

2.

3.

4.

5.

Persuasive: *In one sentence, state what you expect your reader to believe or do as a result of reading your essay.*

For example:

As the destruction of Pompeii in 79 C.E. illustrated nearly two millennia ago, humans have not tamed nature and should stop considering areas prone to natural disasters "prime real estate" and putting countless human lives in harm's way.

1.

2.

3.

4.

5.

Brainstorming Points of Elaboration

Think about the *purpose* of each thesis you drafted in Exercise 2. The first set was simply to convey some information—purely informational writing. The second set was expressive, offering an opinion or insight on the topic without calling on your reader to act or change his or her own view. The third set is persuasive. You explicitly want to sway your reader's opinion or convince him or her to take action.

The expansion of each thesis into an essay demands a different type of development, information of a different quality and character.

Exercise 3: Identifying Required Information

Choose one thesis for each of the three purposes in Exercise 2 and list the types of information you would need to support this thesis and where you might find that information. Remember that you need information to:
- *explain precisely what you mean.*
- *establish your credibility as a person whose opinion is worth the reader's consideration.*
- *prove that your thesis is true and accurate.*

For example:

Informational Thesis:
Although the eruption of Mount Vesuvius that destroyed the city of Pompeii in the year 79 C.E., surprised tens of thousands of people and led to their deaths, the eruption did not occur without warning, and many lives could have been saved had those warnings been heeded.

Information You Need:
- *What warning signs did the residents have? (especially dates and nature of events)*
- *What could residents have done to save their lives?*
- *Were the warning signs observed? Debated? What had been decided?*
- *Did anyone escape?*
- *What eyewitness/survivor accounts are available, and what do they say about the surprise eruption?*

For example:
Expressive Thesis:
The most important lesson to be learned from the massive loss of life during the destruction of Pompeii in the year 79 C.E. is that humans cannot afford to be complacent and overconfident in their attempts to conquer nature.

Information You Need:
- *Why was Pompeii built near the foot of a volcano?*
- *Was Vesuvius known to be still active? What was its eruption history?*
- *What was the statistical probability of a major eruption?*
- *Did weather factors, such as wind, play a role in city's destruction?*
- *If Vesuvius had erupted in another direction, what (if anything) would have been damaged?*
- *Could the city have been built somewhere else to make it safer? Where?*
- *Did the layout of the city contribute in any way to the disaster?*
- *How could the city have been made safer?*
- *What warning signs did the residents have before the 79 C.E., eruption? (Especially dates and nature of events)*
- *Were the warning signs observed? Debated? What had been decided?*

For example:

Persuasive Thesis:

As the destruction of Pompeii in 79 C.E., illustrated nearly two millennia ago, humans have not tamed nature and should stop considering areas prone to natural disasters "prime real estate", putting countless human lives in harm's way.

Information You Need:

- *Why was Pompeii built near the foot of a volcano?*
- *Was there a need for a city at that exact location?*
- *Was Vesuvius known to be still active? What was its eruption history?*
- *What was the statistical probability of a major eruption?*
- *Could the city have been built somewhere else to make it safer? Where?*
- *What other (more recent) catastrophes are the result of inhabiting dangerous areas? (Especially Katrina and Rita damage in the Gulf Coast in 2005).*
- *What other threats of natural disasters seem imminent? (Especially a major hurricane hitting Long Island and the San Andreas fault in California).*

1. **Informational Thesis:**

Information You Need:

2. **Expressive Thesis:**

Information You Need:

3. **Persuasive Thesis:**

Information You Need:

Development and Elaboration Through Research

Throughout your life, the need to find information and report on what you learned through your own research will appear again and again. If anything, as we progress deeper into the twenty-first century, the need to perform independent information searches will increase. The abundance of questionable information sources will likely increase as well.

Review: Evaluating Potential Sources

Remember that research is the process of identifying information you need and gathering it from enough valid sources to give you sufficient support for a complete and credible discussion.

In previous books, you've worked on taking good notes and determining whether or not a particular source is worth your time. You have *no* chance of making a strong case or establishing your own credentials as an expert if you present faulty evidence from flawed sources.

There are several factors that you should use to determine a potential source's reliability:

1. the source's identity.

   Except in a few, rare cases, you need to know—and present to your reader— the **name** of the author of the material. Any information from an anonymous or unnamed source should be held suspect.

   Even if the name is published, often the source gives no information about the author's **title or position**. You might know that the information came from Jill Hampton-Smythe, but is Ms. Hampton-Smythe an archaeologist? A journalist? A high school teacher? So Jill Hampton-Smythe might present all sorts of wonderful information about the eruption of Mount Vesuvius and the fall of Pompeii, but if Ms. Hampton-Smythe is a travel agent, then much of what she has to say is probably of questionable validity.

2. the source's **credentials** (Notice that credibility and credentials both come from the same Latin root that means "believe" or "trust").

    Knowing the name and title or position of a source is still not sufficient since the name and title offer no guarantee of the potential source's competence or integrity. What is the source's **educational background**? What **degrees or certificates** does he or she have? In what fields? What **actual experience** does he or she have in the area you are researching? **Who else recommends** this source as valuable, and what are *this* person's credentials? Call it snobbery, but it is likely that the opinion of the director of the United States Department of Natural Resources and Environmental Control on global warming is probably going to carry more weight than your high school teacher's opinion on the same subject.

3. the source's affiliations.

    Always beware of bias. Always be aware that everyone is, to some extent, biased. So, we know **Jarvis Simpson** is a **Ph.D., in Environmental Science,** and is the **director of the United States Department of Natural Resources and Environmental Control**. That would establish his credentials as a valid source for factual information. When stating an opinion, however, is his opinion colored by his own **political** or **religious** affiliation? To what extent do Jarvis Simpson's **ties to the current presidential administration** affect how he views environmental issues?

Note: when it comes to the issue of bias, it is not necessary to discredit a source completely because of perceived bias—*all* sources are going to be biased in one way or another—but it *is* important to be aware of the source's bias and to deal with it, either by simply acknowledging it or by citing another source whose biases lie in the other direction.

However: when a source's bias is so strong that he or she distorts or ignores facts, accidentally or intentionally commits any of the logical fallacies discussed in the second book in this series, blatantly ridicules those who disagree with him or her, or in any other way seems too reactionary or extremist, you should *avoid* this source.

Also keep in mind the factors that you need to use to determine a potential source's authority:

- How many levels of approval and revision did the information pass through before arriving in your hands? The more "filters" information has had to pass, the more authoritative the source is likely to be. One technical term for review and approval of imfprmation is "vetting."

Keep in mind:

- Much of the Internet has **no vetting**. Anyone can (and many do) post fabricated information just to undermine students' research papers.

- Television and radio have **a few filters**. The more recent the information or news, the more likely it is to be unchallenged, untested, and biased or inaccurate.

- The print news media have **a few more filters.** Newspaper articles must pass through one or more levels of approval before finding their way into print. **Be careful, however, not to confuse news and information with entertainment or editorials.**

- Finally, the book publishing industry has the **most vetted information**. Competition makes the market highly selective, and legitimate publishers can take the time to make certain what they publish is accurate. **Beware, of course, of self-published (and electronically-published) material or material that comes from a publishing house that obviously has an agenda beyond sharing accurate and objective information.**

Even in the twenty-first century—print sources are still better than Internet sources.

Review: Evaluating Internet Sources

The three "Open Domains" are so called because there are *no* restrictions on who may register under these domains:

.com designates the site of a commercial business. At some level, the site exists to make a profit, not merely to provide information.

.net specifies an information network. Consider a *.net* site to be a commercial site.

.org signifies a nonprofit organization. Be prepared for the information to reflect the organization's acknowledged (and often unacknowledged) biases. For example, the National Rifle Association is firmly and publicly opposed to most forms of gun control legislation, while Mothers Against Drunk Driving supports imposing severe sentences on drivers who injure others while intoxicated.

One problem with the *.com*, *.net*, and *.org* domains is that *any* type of information can be found at these sites. Most personal blogs are in the *.com* and *.net* domains, and just about *any* organization can apply for, and be granted, a *.org* domain, even if the organization's sole purpose is to propagandize its view and advance its agenda.

Then, there are the restricted domains:

.edu designates a degree-granting institution of higher education that is accredited by one of the six U.S. regional accrediting agencies.[1] This includes community colleges.

.mil is restricted to the military of the United States of America.

.gov specifies the site of an agency of the federal government of the United States of America.

.int is the domain of international organizations like NATO (North Atlantic Treaty Organization).

---

[1]Middle States Association of Colleges and Schools, New England Association of Schools and Colleges, North Central Association of Colleges and Schools, Northwest Commission on Colleges and Universities, Southern Association of Colleges and Schools, Western Association of Schools and Colleges

The restrictions regarding *who* may post information on these domains eliminates many of the concerns you should have regarding bias and accuracy in non-restricted domains. Still, every organization—whether public, private, local, or international—wants to present information that supports its own goals.

For example, former Vice President Al Gore presents a lot of excellent science in his film on global warming. He also presents a lot of politics. Your job as researcher is to be able to recognize which is which and to know how to deal with it.

This is what good research entails.

Exercise 4: Evaluating Sources

Each of the following is an excerpt from a fictional article about a fictional social/ political issue. Read each excerpt, consider where the information came from, who the source of the information is, and determine how likely you would be to use that information (or any other information on the case from that source). After you have evaluated the source, explain why you have evaluated it as you have.

Evaluate each source on a scale of 1–10, with 10 being a highly credible and authoritative source you would definitely use, and 1 being a highly questionable source you would not even consider using.

1. From: http://www.freetheeasternshore.org

The State Of Delmarva represents the great themes of American history. The same issues that impelled the signers of the Declaration of Independence to draft their historic document underlie the desire of the good people of the Eastern Shore to separate themselves from indifferent governments and ally themselves with friends. The same feeling of isolation from the government and lack of representation that our colonial forefathers endured we now endure.

We are a nation founded upon the principles of revolution. What could be more revolutionary than unhappy citizens wanting to form their own state? Why, after all, did we secede from England and form our own country? Because we felt we were not being represented fairly!

Many people, even in our own states, think we are joking, but this is a very serious matter to those of us who want the same services and facilities that the voters and taxpayers in other parts of the state take for granted. Previous attempts did not succeed, and the needs of the impoverished rural areas of Maryland's and Virginia's Eastern shores are still not addressed by the state governments. Obviously, the concerns of citizens in Accomack County, Virginia, or Cecil County, Maryland, are not the same as those in the Washington, D.C., suburbs of either state. But that is not to say that their concerns are any less valid.

Rating:

Explanation:

2. From: Havrad, Jacob, Esq. "Studies in Little-Known Constitutional Provisions" *Constitution Quarterly.* October—December 2006: 2135-2257.

While seeming to prohibit the formation of a new state by secession and/or recombination of already-existing states, Article IV, Section 3 of the Constitution actually establishes the conditions under which a recombination like this can occur: "no new State shall be formed or erected within the Jurisdiction of any other State; nor any State be formed by the Junction of two or more States, or Parts of States, without the Consent of the Legislatures of the States concerned as well as of the Congress."

Rating:

Explanation:

3. From: http://www.randy'srantings.com, personal blog of Randolph Cripps, proud, twelfth-generation Delawarean

No one in Delaware supports this initiative. Delaware has a strong economy (less than 10% unemployment), good schools (almost all of our schools are rated "above average" or higher by the United States Department of Education), and is just a nice place to live (no air or water pollution, no sales tax, and the lowest crime rate in the United States). Why would we want to take on the problems of foreigners from other states? And since Delaware is a *whole* state, why should we cease to exist and allow ourselves to be subsumed into this mega-state of Delmarva? If the folks in Virginia's and Maryland's Eastern Shores are so unhappy with their current status, let them secede and form their own state. Leave Delaware out of it.

Rating:

Explanation:

4. From: "Secessionist Committee Abducted by Aliens in Nation's Capital" *Weekly World Enquirer.* 19 December 2006.

The seventy-two hours during which an *ad hoc* committee of independent businessmen and women from the Virginia and Maryland Eastern Shore apparently disappeared while visiting Washington, D.C., have finally been accounted for.

"We was taken aboard a big spaceship," reports Rufus McIntyre, a commercial fisherman from a small island town in Northampton County, Virginia. McIntyre told an *Enquirer* reporter, "I was given a shot that numbed my whole body, and then I was probed and prodded like a science experiment!"

Other members of the committee, who were in Washington, D.C., to present to Congress their petition to be allowed to secede from the states of Maryland and Virginia and join with tiny Delaware to form the State of Delmarva, would not comment on Mr. McIntyre's claims.

"I cannot account for those lost seventy-two hours," Magda Rosario of Salzburg, Maryland, insisted. "We'd left the House chambers and were walking back to our hotel. The next thing we knew, it was nighttime and we were standing on the corner of Wisconsin and Avenue D. We were all really tired and hungry, and some of us had pounding headaches." Ms. Rosario is a massage therapist and owns an alternative medicine supply store in downtown Salzburg.

Other committee members, who asked that their names not be divulged, reported their fears that their petition would not be taken seriously if it were believed that they were crazy or had somehow gotten involved in some shady dealings while on their political junket. "I'd hate to see the issue of statehood for Delmarva die because some bug-eyed goons just had to have a glimpse at the type of stock we're made of here in the Eastern Shore," McIntyre concluded. "It just ain't right."

Rating:

Explanation:

5. From: http://www.lawskoolnow.com

ADVERTISEMENT: Earn your law degree in six weeks—
GUARANTEED! (six-week period begins after completion
of three- to four-year period of course work). Some of our
nation's biggest-named lawyers attended our correspondence
law school and have handled such high-profile cases as
McGuffey and Reeder v Oxbow Press and The People of the
Eastern Shores of Maryland and Virginia v. the Maryland and
Virginia State Legislatures! ("Big-name" is defined as five
or more letters for the first name and seven or more letters
for the surname.) Call ------- for your free information packet
(One-time postage and perusal fee of $75 not included).

Rating:

Explanation:

6. From: http://www.departmentofstatesrights.gov

Notes on the Formation of The State of Jefferson, The United
States' Forty-Ninth State

- In 1852, a bill was introduced in the California State
  Legislature for portions of northern California and southern
  Oregon to be formed into a single state to be called
  Jefferson.
- In 1941, the issue arose again when certain counties in
  northern California and southern Oregon decided that they
  were not being fairly represented by their respective state
  capitals.
- These counties included: Siskiyou, Del Norte, and Modoc
  Counties in California; and Curry, Josephine, and Jackson
  Counties in Oregon.
- Poor roads and a lack of bridges made it difficult for the
  area's industries to function.
- The Chamber of Commerce in Yreka, California, persuaded
  the Siskiyou County Board of Supervisors to look into the
  possibility of forming a 49th state.

- They wanted to name the new state "Mittelwestcoastia."
- *The Siskiyou Daily News* ran a contest to name the new state.
- Entries included: "Orofino," "Bonanza," "Del Curiskiyou," "Siskardelmo," "New West," "New Hope," "Discontent" and "Jefferson."
- "Jefferson" won, and the man who submitted the name was awarded two dollars.
- Every Thursday, members of "The State of Jefferson Citizens Committee" would go out to Highway 99 where it entered the boundaries of Jefferson, and cover road signs with sheets that said "State of Jefferson" on them.
    o They set up roadblocks and patrolled on horse-back with guns.
    o They stopped traffic and handed out copies of the "Proclamation of Independence," along with red and blue stickers that read, "I have visited JEFFERSON, the 49th State."
- A California legislator insulted the protesting counties by commenting that the northern counties "bartered in bear claws and eagle beaks."
- Yreka, California was designated "Temporary State Capital."
- On December 4, 1941, Yrekans held an election for the first provisional governor of the State of Jefferson.
- Residents dressed as cowboys and toted pistols and rifles as they again handed out leaflets on Highway 99.
- In the parade, many students carried picket signs:
    o "The Promised Land—Our Roads Are Paved With Promises."
    o "If Our Roads You Would Travel, Bring Your Own Gravel."
- December 7, 1941, brought news of the surprise attack on Pearl Harbor, Hawaii.

The Provisional Governor of the State of Jefferson's last act as chief executive was to state, "In view of the National emergency, the acting officers of the Provisional Territory of Jefferson here and now discontinue any and all activities. The State of Jefferson was originated for the sole purpose of calling the attention of the proper authorities...to the fact we have immense deposits of strategic and necessary defense minerals and that we need roads to develop those. We have accomplished that purpose and henceforth all of our efforts will be directed toward assisting our States and Federal Government in the...

Rating:

Explanation:

7. From: Miller, Lisa-Anne. "America's Fifty-First State?" *Journal of American History.* 31 October 2006: 25-30.

The part of Maryland east of the Chesapeake Bay, known as the Eastern Shore, includes more than one third of the State of Maryland's land area (but less than one-tenth of its population) and nine of Maryland's twenty-three counties, specifically: Caroline, Cecil, Dorchester, Kent, Queen Anne's, Somerset, Talbot, Wicomico, and Worcester Counties.

Eastern Shore Virginia is considerably smaller and even less populated, containing two Virginia counties: Accomack and Northampton. Residents of both Eastern Shore regions have long complained that their interests—so vastly different from the majority populations on the mainlands of their respective states—are neither understood nor represented by Annapolis and Richmond, the capitals of the states involved in the controversy.

Nor is the secession movement new. Eastern Shore Maryland petitioned the Maryland General Assembly for the right to secede in 1833, 1835, 1852 and as recently as 1999. The 1999 petition indicated that the Eastern Shore desired to form its own state. The earlier proposals suggested combination of the Eastern Shores of Maryland and Virginia with the state of Delaware to form a new state—Delmarva.

Rating:

Explanation:

8. From: Macintoch, Nathaniel, Hon. *The Irony of a Government Of, By, and For the "People."* Newkirk: State University of Delaware Press, 2006.

The formation of a new state from the remnants of one or more divided states is provided for in the Constitution. But it is not easy, and the reason attempts like the Delmarva Initiative failed in the past is that those who are most disillusioned with their state governments and desiring change are exactly those least able to navigate the rocky waters of state and federal politics.

First of all, would-be secessionists first need the approval of their respective state legislatures. How ironic that the body accused of caring least about a region's best interests must be petitioned to act *in* that region's best interests, even if at some cost to itself. Most secessionists, seeking fairness, are ill-prepared to barter: how can an underrepresented farmer or fisherman hope to convince the legislature that the loss of tax revenue and Congressional representation—the inevitable results of allowing a region to secede—are *good things?* How can a hardworking, simple man hope to match wits and oily tongues against polished politicians? The naïve citizen, who has already been poorly served by his government, must now ask that government to sacrifice itself for him.

Yet, even if a ragtag band of locals succeeds in securing its legislature's permission to form its own state, this *ersatz* committee must now petition the Congress of the United States for permission to govern itself. If appearing before the state legislature was a daunting task, imagine how much more formidable the icons of Capitol Hill must seem.

It is little wonder that United States history provides us with scant attempts at state re-formation, and even fewer examples of a successful endeavor.

Rating:

Explanation:

Exercise 5: Development and Elaboration: Using Other Content Areas

Consider what you are currently studying in your other academic classes and do the following:

Note an idea or concept you've studied this week with which you agree.

Note an idea or concept you've studied this week with which you disagree.

Note an idea or concept you've studied this week which you find especially interesting.

Note an idea or concept you've studied this week which you do not fully understand.

For the idea or concept with which you agree, answer the following questions:

How much do you know about this subject?

What is the basis of your agreement?

What evidence can you offer to support your opinion?

List the source(s) for this evidence:

What evidence exists to support the opposite opinion?

List the source(s) for this evidence:

How can you refute that evidence?

For the idea or concept with which you disagree, answer the following questions:

How much do you know about this subject?

What is the basis of your disagreement?

What evidence can you offer to support your opinion?

List the source(s) for this evidence:

What evidence exists to support the opposite opinion?

List the source(s) for this evidence:

How can you refute that evidence?

For the idea or concept you find particularly interesting, answer the following questions:

Is this new knowledge or something you knew before?

What do you find interesting about it?

What background information would you have to give to a reader in order to explain this?

Writing Opportunity: *The Writing Assessment Essay: The AP and/or Writing Placement Exam*

Remember that the writing portions of most assessments and national exams are designed to evaluate your ability to organize your thoughts and communicate them in a reasonably clear fashion. Many of these exams also measure your ability to look at a piece of literature, such as a short story or poem, read and analyze it, and develop a reasonable response without the benefit of teacher instruction or classroom discussion.

Finally, these assessments also measure—to a somewhat lesser extent—your command of the conventions of standard written English.

Keeping in mind the time constraints associated with this type of essay, the key to success is choosing and developing an idea as fully as you can as quickly as you can. *All* of the traits of powerful essays are important in a writing assessment, but—while your scorer may be instructed to forgive the occasional spelling or grammatical error—you will be heavily penalized if you have nothing to say or if you do not discuss your topic fully. Therefore, *Development* and *Elaboration* is probably the most important trait in this setting.

Below is a writing prompt similar to ones you are likely to encounter on the Advanced Placement in English Literature and Composition[2] exam or in a college-freshman-level English assessment designed to determine which freshman English course you should take.

Remember to apply the techniques you learned in this Trait to develop a main idea and then offer as many supporting points and specific details in support of that main idea as you can.

---

[2]Advanced Placement is a registered trademark of The College Board, which neither sponsors nor endorses this product

Prompt: Read the following short story, written several years after the publication of *The Red Badge of Courage*, and write a well-organized essay discussing the ways in which the author's style (diction, syntax, tone, selection of detail, etc.) reveals his attitude about Henry Fleming.

The Veteran
by Stephen Crane

Out of the low window could be seen three hickory trees placed irregularly in a meadow that was resplendent in spring-time green. Farther away, the old, dismal belfry of the village church loomed over the pines. A horse, meditating in the shade of one of the hickories, lazily
5 swished his tail. The warm sunshine made an oblong of vivid yellow on the floor of the grocery.

"Could you see the whites of their eyes?" said the man, who was seated on a soap box.

"Nothing of the kind," replied old Henry warmly. "Just a lot of flitting
10 figures, and I let go at where they 'peared to be the thickest. Bang!"

"Mr. Fleming," said the grocer—his deferential voice expressed somehow the old man's exact social weight—"Mr. Fleming, you never was frightened much in them battles, was you?"

The veteran looked down and grinned. Observing his manner, the
15 entire group tittered. "Well, I guess I was," he answered finally. "Pretty well scared, sometimes. Why, in my first battle I thought the sky was falling down. I thought the world was coming to an end. You bet I was scared."

Every one laughed. Perhaps it seemed strange and rather wonderful
20 to them that a man should admit the thing, and in the tone of their laughter there was probably more admiration than if old Fleming had declared that he had always been a lion. Moreover, they knew that he had ranked as an orderly sergeant, and so their opinion of his heroism was fixed. None, to be sure, knew how an orderly sergeant ranked, but
25 then it was understood to be somewhere just shy of a major-general's stars. So, when old Henry admitted that he had been frightened, there was a laugh.

"The trouble was," said the old man, "I thought they were all shooting at me. Yes, sir, I thought every man in the other army was
30 aiming at me in particular, and only me. And it seemed so darned

unreasonable, you know. I wanted to explain to 'em what an almighty good fellow I was, because I thought then they might quit all trying to hit me. But I couldn't explain, and they kept on being unreasonable—blim!—blam! bang! So I run!"

35   Two little triangles of wrinkles appeared at the corners of his eyes. Evidently he appreciated some comedy in this recital. Down near his feet, however, little Jim, his grandson, was visibly horror-stricken. His hands were clasped nervously, and his eyes were wide with astonishment at this terrible scandal, his most magnificent grandfather

40   telling such a thing.

"That was at Chancellorsville. Of course, afterward I got kind of used to it. A man does. Lots of men, though, seem to feel all right from the start. I did, as soon as I 'got on to it,' as they say now; but at first I was pretty well flustered. Now, there was young Jim Conklin, old

45   Si Conklin's son—that used to keep the tannery—you none of you recollect him—well, he went into it from the start just as if he was born to it. But with me it was different. I had to get used to it."

When little Jim walked with his grandfather he was in the habit of skipping along on the stone pavement, in front of the three stores and

50   the hotel of the town, and betting that he could avoid the cracks. But upon this day he walked soberly, with his hand gripping two of his grandfather's fingers. Sometimes he kicked abstractedly at dandelions that curved over the walk. Any one could see that he was much troubled.

55   "There's Sickles's colt over in the medder, Jimmie," said the old man. "Don't you wish you owned one like him?"

"Um," said the boy, with a strange lack of interest. He continued his reflections. Then finally he ventured: "Grandpa—now—was that true what you was telling those men?"

60   "What?" asked the grandfather. "What was I telling them?"

"Oh, about your running."

"Why yes, that was true enough, Jimmie. It was my first fight, and there was an awful lot of noise, you know."

Jimmie seemed dazed that this idol, of its own will, should so totter. His

65   stout boyish idealism was injured.

Presently the grandfather said: "Sickles's colt is going for a drink. Don't you wish you owned Sickles's colt, Jimmie?"

The boy merely answered: "He ain't as nice as our'n." He lapsed then into another moody silence.

70   One of the hired men, a Swede, desired to drive to the county seat
for purposes of his own. The old man loaned a horse and an unwashed
buggy. It appeared later that one of the purposes of the Swede was to
get drunk.

After quelling some boisterous frolic of the farm hands and boys in
75   the garret, the old man had that night gone peacefully to sleep, when
he was aroused by clamoring at the kitchen door. He grabbed his
trousers, and they waved out behind as he dashed forward. He could
hear the voice of the Swede, screaming and blubbering. He pushed
the wooden button, and, as the door flew open, the Swede, a maniac,
80   stumbled inward, chattering, weeping, still screaming: "De barn fire!
Fire! Fire! De barn fire! Fire! Fire! Fire!"

There was a swift and indescribable change in the old man. His face
ceased instantly to be a face; it became a mask, a grey thing, with
horror written about the mouth and eyes. He hoarsely shouted at the
85   foot of the little rickety stairs, and immediately, it seemed, there came
down an avalanche of men. No one knew that during this time the
old lady had been standing in her night-clothes at the bedroom door
yelling: "What's th' matter? What's th' matter? What's th' matter?"

When they dashed toward the barn, it presented to their eyes its
90   usual appearance, solemn, rather mystic in the black night. The Swede's
lantern was overturned at a point some yards in front of the barn doors.
It contained a wild little conflagration of its own, and even in their
excitement some of those who ran felt a gentle secondary vibration of
the thrifty part of their minds at sight of this overturned lantern. Under
95   ordinary circumstances it would have been a calamity.

But the cattle in the barn were trampling, trampling, trampling,
and above this noise could be heard a humming like the song of
innumerable bees. The old man hurled aside the great doors, and a
yellow flame leaped out at one corner and sped and wavered frantically
100   up the old grey wall. It was glad, terrible, this single flame, like the wild
banner of deadly and triumphant foes.

The motley crowd from the garret had come with all the pails of
the farm. They flung themselves upon the well. It was a leisurely old
machine, long dwelling in indolence. It was in the habit of giving out
105   water with a sort of reluctance. The men stormed at it, cursed it; but
it continued to allow the buckets to be filled only after the wheezy
windlass had howled many protests at the mad-handed men.

With his opened knife in his hand old Fleming himself had gone
headlong into the barn, where the stifling smoke swirled with the air

110 currents, and where could be heard in its fullness the terrible chorus of the flames, laden with tones of hate and death, a hymn of wonderful ferocity.

He flung a blanket over an old mare's head, cut the halter close to

115 the manager, led the mare to the door, and fairly kicked her out to safety. He returned with the same blanket, and rescued one of the work horses. He took five horses out, and then came out himself, with his clothes bravely on fire. He had no whiskers, and very little hair on his head. They soused five pailfuls of water on him. His eldest son made a

120 clean miss with the sixth pailful, because the old man had turned and was running down the decline and around to the basement of the barn, where were the stanchions of the cows. Some one noticed at the time that he ran very lamely, as if one of the frenzied horses had smashed his hip.

125 The cows, with their heads held in the heavy stanchions, had thrown themselves, strangled themselves, tangled themselves—done everything which the ingenuity of their exuberant fear could suggest to them.

Here, as at the well, the same thing happened to every man save

130 one. Their hands went mad. They became incapable of everything save the power to rush into dangerous situations.

The old man released the cow nearest the door, and she, blind drunk with terror, crashed into the Swede. The Swede had been running to and fro babbling. He carried an empty milk-pail, to which he clung with

135 an unconscious, fierce enthusiasm. He shrieked like one lost as he went under the cow's hoofs, and the milk-pail, rolling across the floor, made a flash of silver in the gloom.

Old Fleming took a fork, beat off the cow, and dragged the paralyzed Swede to the open air. When they had rescued all the cows save one,

140 which had so fastened herself that she could not be moved an inch, they returned to the front of the barn, and stood sadly, breathing like men who had reached the final point of human effort.

Many people had come running. Some one had even gone to the church, and now, from the distance, rang the tocsin note of the old

145 bell. There was a long flare of crimson on the sky, which made remote people speculate as to the whereabouts of the fire.

The long flames sang their drumming chorus in voices of the heaviest bass. The wind whirled clouds of smoke and cinders into the faces of the spectators. The form of the old barn was outlined in black amid

150 these masses of orange-hued flames.

And then came this Swede again, crying as one who is the weapon of the sinister fates: "De colts! De colts! You have forgot de colts!"

Old Fleming staggered. It was true: they had forgotten the two colts in the box-stalls at the back of the barn. "Boys," he said, "I must try to
155   get 'em out."

They clamored about him then, afraid for him, afraid of what they should see. Then they talked wildly each to each. "Why, it's sure death!" "He would never get out!" "Why it's suicide for a man to go in there!"
160   Old Fleming stared absent-mindedly at the open doors. "The poor little things!" he said. He rushed into the barn.

When the roof fell in, a great funnel of smoke swarmed toward the sky, as if the old man's mighty spirit, released from its body—a little bottle—had swelled like the genie of fable. The smoke was tinted rose-
165   hue from the flames, and perhaps the unutterable midnights of the universe will have no power to daunt the color of this soul.

Step 1: *Develop your thesis*

What is Crane's attitude toward Henry Fleming? How does he convey this attitude? State your answers to these questions in a single sentence (two at the most).

Step 2: *Brainstorm your supporting ideas*

The prompt to which you are responding asks you to discuss the general quality of "style," but then specifies diction, syntax, tone, and selection of detail as elements of style to be considered. Your ideas should, therefore, first and foremost, try to show how one or more of these specified traits helps to convey Crane's attitude.

When you venture beyond the above list for more ideas, make certain that the elements you choose to discuss are indeed elements of style. Plot structure, for example, and character development techniques, are *not* usually considered aspects of a writer's style in the same way that narrative point of view or license with language conventions might be.

Step 3: *Examine the text for evidence and examples*

If you are allowed to, it would be easiest to simply underline or bracket the words, phrases, etc., you are going to use as support or evidence for your points. If you cannot do this, simply take notes with line numbers and a few key words for each quotation.

Remember that *every* point you want to establish about a particular element of style and its contribution to Crane's message *must* be illustrated and supported by *at least two examples* drawn directly from the story. If you cannot find at least two examples, then the point you are trying to make is probably not valid.

Time Clue: The Advanced Placement exam instructions recommend 40 minutes for a single essay. You are also likely to have less than an hour for an English placement exam as well. Therefore, you should give yourself no more than 10–15 minutes for these first three steps.

Step 4: *Organize a quick outline or graphic organizer*

Most likely the aspects of style you are going to discuss will be your main idea headings. You don't need to copy *all* of your support or evidence, but you do need to indicate in what order you will present your material from the story: In the same order as it appears in the story? Order of importance or impact? Chronologically?

Time Clue: Don't use more than 3–5 minutes for your outline. It is more important for you to make the decisions you need to make regarding the order in which you will discuss the various elements and the order in which you will present your support.

Step 5: *Draft your essay*

Chances are, this will be your *only* draft—so make it good. Remember that the level of freshman English course you are assigned to might be determined by the quality of this essay.

You have already listed your examples, so this is merely framing them into sentences and paragraphs.

> **Time Clue:** Give yourself 10–15 minutes for this step. If you did a good enough job in Steps 2 and 3, writing these paragraphs will be a breeze.

Step 6: *Reread and revise your essay*

If time allows, go back and double-check your essay, at least to clean up any spelling or minor grammatical errors you may find. You probably won't have time for a full second draft, so be sure to take the time to make this draft as "clean" as possible.

Applying
the
SECOND Truth

Powerful writing is understandable to others.

3
Simple Truths
and

6
Essential Traits
of

Powerful Writing

Organization

Trait
Two

TRAIT TWO:

ORGANIZATION

Unity and Coherence

Remember that the two key issues to consider when organizing a long, complex work are *unity* and *coherence*. Unity is the quality that *every sentence in a paragraph* and *every paragraph in an essay or paper* relates to a single topic.

Coherence deals with *how* the individual parts relate to the whole.

Make Yours Better!

First there were eight. Then there were nine. Then there were eight again. Then there were twelve. Finally, there were eight and three dwarfs. We're talking about planets, of course, and a debate has been raging since 1930, when Pluto was first discovered, about whether this tiny chunk of ice was, or a planet.

From the very beginning, Pluto's designation as the ninth planet was debated. It simply was too odd to be a true planet. While the other eight planets orbit the sun in essentially the same plane, Pluto's orbit is a full 17% off. The orbits of the other eight planets are essentially round, while Pluto's is "eccentric," oval-shaped, with the sun not at its center. In fact, at the point in orbit when it is closest to the sun, it is actually closer than the eighth planet, Neptune. This means that Pluto's orbit actually crosses Neptune's— and no other planet has an orbit like this.

Still, many early twentieth-century astronomers had been searching for over a decade for a ninth planet, and when Pluto was observed, they were all too willing to admit the tiny oddball into the club.

As early as 1978, however, Pluto's identity as a planet had been called into question. Some famous planetariums, in fact, refused to include Pluto in their charts and models of the solar system. The issue back then was the discovery of Charon, another body that exhibited some of the characteristics of a planet and some of the characteristics of a moon. As other Pluto-like objects were discovered in Pluto's neighborhood, most notably a body called 2003 UB313 (nicknamed Xena), most astronomers argued that, if Pluto was

- The first paragraph seems to introduce a discussion of a debate. We expect to be asked to consider the pros and cons of the issue.

- To begin with historical background is tempting, but not necessarily the best organization. Points of argument are implied, but not really laid out for the reader.

- The essay still focuses on historical background. It needs to reveal the purpose.

a planet, so was Xena. If Xena was not, neither was Pluto.

Finally, the debate reached a head in August of 2006, when members of the International Astronomical Union met in Prague, Czech Republic. The main topic: What is a planet, and is Pluto one? One of the earliest definitions drafted on August 16 allowed Pluto to retain its planetary status, but would have also admitted three other bodies into the clique. Ceres, a body in the asteroid belt between Mars and Jupiter, would become a planet, as would Pluto's former moon, Charon, and the notorious Xena.

Finally, on August 22, a final definition was approved that demoted Charon, Ceres, Xena, and Pluto to the status of "dwarf planet." Thus, the solar system is now composed of eight planets and three dwarfs—pending any future discoveries. The final straw in Pluto's demotion was that Pluto had failed to "clear its neighborhood" of debris, which means that Pluto's gravitation has not sufficiently either attracted or repelled rocks, comets, and other space junk so that it is essentially the only body to occupy its orbital plane.

Whether Pluto is a planet or a dwarf, whether Ceres is an asteroid or a dwarf, and whether Xena becomes an official name or she is christened something more legitimate, not much is going to change here on Earth. The sun will still rise in the East, set in the West, and the tilt of the axis will still determine our seasons. Still, there are those who feel as though something important, some archetype, has been lost. If something that three or more generations of school children have taken for granted can be declared incorrect by a simple majority vote, what other essential truths can be denied? Should we still look both ways before we cross the street?

■ One major point of the debate is expressed. The passage has been interesting and relatively easy to follow, but has not really delivered on what the first paragraph suggested was going to follow.

■ The essay ends on a philosophical note. A follow-up dialogue is invited, but this is not the inevitable conclusion to the passage as written.

Essay Critique

There is nothing wrong with the organizational pattern of this essay. The historical background of the debate is presented in chronological order. The introduction might not be tightened up to better represent the author's purpose. More space should be dedicated to the characteristics of planets that were debated. If the passage ends on a philosophical note, then the fact that this is a *reflection* more so than a debate should be clarified earlier.

This essay receives a score of 10 on the:

Organization Rubric

14 = ACCOMPLISHED
The **organizational plan** of the essay seems inevitable given the topic, purpose, and audience.

13 = The **essay flows** so that the reader gets a sense of where the discussion is leading and understands how it has been put together.

12 = The **structure of** the essay helps the reader understand the information and follow the point.

11 = The **organizational plan** is clear, original, and logical. It does not detract from the reader's appreciation of the discussion, but does not enhance it either.

10 = PROFICIENT
The **organizational plan** of the essay is clear and original, and appropriate; but is not necessarily the best plan for the subject, purpose, and audience.

Reviewing the Principles of Unity and Coherence

The following essay contains a lot of information. Much of it, however, is irrelevant and leads the reader off on tangents so that the main idea and the author's purpose become lost:

Chemically, it's called *cyanoacrylate*. Generically, it's called "super glue," and it's sold under such trademarked brand names as *KrazyGlue*™. Nearly every household in America has a bottle, and nearly everyone who's ever used it has a tale to tell. Some of the stories of unfortunate accidental gluings would lead one to the conclusion that super glue is a menace to society and should never have been released into the general public. When you look beyond the hype and examine the truth of most of these claims, however, you begin to realize that super glue is no more dangerous than the library paste or rubber cement it replaces.

After all, a person could wrap a length of kite string around his neck and strangle himself, so does that mean we should take kite string off the market? And how many accidental electrocutions are there every year? Clearly we must stop the production and consumption of electricity immediately.

There are, of course, the horribly embarrassing stories of the men and women who had the grave misfortune of sitting on a public toilet seat that someone had smeared with superglue. Variations of this urban legend range from having the paramedics remove the seat and parading the humiliated victim through the store to the ambulance to the victim's freeing himself or herself and walking through a crowded restaurant to find help. One British version of the story has the hapless victim push the "button" and set off the "alarm" while stuck in the stall.

Other urban legends have to do with exploding biscuit tubes, and car hoods dented by misdirected elephants. Basically, an urban legend is anything that is currently in the oral tradition, exists in numerous versions, all of which have actually happened to someone who knows someone who knows the person who is telling the tale. In order to be an urban legend, the tale must be purported to be true.

Blatant hoaxes, like warnings about non-existent computer viruses, or the desire of a supposedly dying youngster to be in the Guinness Book of World Records for having the most post cards from all over the world can sometimes cause nuisances. The problem with the latter hoax was that it inundated this tiny post office in Scotland with postcards from well-meaning good Samaritans for *years*.

Still, one commonly related superglue mishap is true and occurs frequently: the accidental gluing of inappropriate body parts. Hospital emergency rooms worldwide report a surprisingly high incidence of this type accident. In the United States, some superglue manufacturers feel it necessary to include safety instructions on what to do if a customer were to find him or herself in such a bind.

In 2005, the United States Department of Energy safety practices newsletter described the case of a Department of Energy worker who accidentally squirted superglue into his eyes while trying to unclog the tip. This worker was taken by ambulance to the hospital where he spent "several days" waiting for the glue to "work itself loose." The Department of Energy brochure notes that in most cases of superglue misapplication, no "active treatment" is necessary.

Accidental eye gluings happen all the time, largely because the glue bottles resemble eye-drop bottles. It occurs enough that ophthalmologists have been warning their patients (and asking the glue industry to rethink its packaging) for over sixteen years. In 2001, a team of doctors from the Department of Ophthalmology at the Royal Liverpool University Hospital cited a case in which a mother confused antibiotic eye drops prescribed for her baby's conjunctivitis with fingernail adhesive drops. The mother instilled the superglue into the left eye, which caused eyelash clumping, and a slight abrasion to the child's cornea. This same team cited another case in which a three-year-old saw her mother instill medicinal eye drops. Playing "grown-up," the child imitated her mother's actions, using a dropper of superglue instead of eye drops. Both children received emergency medical treatment and were fine. Even still, the incidence of men, women, and children sealing their eyes shut with their "eye drops" would be alarming until a little research revealed that the glue—while certainly inconvenient and uncomfortable—has been shown to cause damage in very, very, very few cases.

In cases of getting the glue stuck to the inside of your cheek, the "treatment" is simply to let the glue work itself free. Even if the glue were to attach itself directly to the eyeball, according to one brochure, it would detach itself within an hour or to. If you glue your eye or eyes shut, you should flush your eye(s) thoroughly with warm water and cover with a gauze bandage. The glue should work itself out in a few days. The worst harm, it seems, that applying superglue to the human body is that it might burn the skin.

In such cases, the victim is advised to treat the injury like any other burn, after the glue has been removed with warm water. Interestingly, one safety brochure notes that, while it is nearly impossible to swallow superglue (and, thus, poison yourself), it is possible to seal your lips shut! This same brochure notes that it is not likely ever to be necessary to have superglue surgically removed from your body.

Notice how the main idea and the purpose of the essay become clear when unity is restored by removing redundancies and superfluities:

> Chemically, it's called *cyanoacrylate*. Generically, it's called "super glue," and it's sold under such trademarked brand names as *KrazyGlue*™. Nearly every household in America has a bottle, and nearly everyone who's ever used it has a tale to tell. Some of the stories of unfortunate accidental gluings would lead one to the conclusion that super glue is a menace to society and should never have been released into the general public. When you look beyond the hype and examine the truth of most of these claims, however, you begin to realize that super glue is no more dangerous than the library paste or rubber cement it replaces.
>
> ~~After all, a person could wrap a length of kite string around his neck and strangle himself, so does that mean we should take kite string off the market? And how many accidental electrocutions are there every year? Clearly we must stop the production and consumption of electricity immediately.~~
>
> There are, of course, the horribly embarrassing stories of the men and women who had the grave misfortune of sitting on a public toilet seat that someone had smeared with superglue. Variations of this urban legend range from having the paramedics remove the seat and parading the humiliated victim through the store to the ambulance to the victim's freeing himself or herself and walking through a crowded restaurant to find help. One British version of the story has the hapless victim push the "button" and set off the "alarm" while stuck in the stall.
>
> ~~Other urban legends have to do with exploding biscuit tubes, and car hoods dented by misdirected elephants. Basically, an urban legend is anything that is currently in the oral tradition, exists in numerous versions, all of which have actually happened to someone who knows someone who knows the person who is telling the tale. In order to be an urban legend, the tale must be purported to be true.~~
>
> ~~Blatant hoaxes, like warnings about non-existent computer viruses, or the desire of a supposedly dying youngster to be in the Guinness Book of World Records for having the most post cards from all over the world can sometimes cause nuisances. The problem with that hoax was that it inundated this tiny post office in Scotland with postcards from well-meaning good Samaritans for years.~~
>
> Still, one commonly related superglue mishap is true and occurs frequently: the accidental gluing of inappropriate body parts. Hospital emergency rooms worldwide report a surprisingly high incidence of this type accident. In the United States, some superglue manufacturers feel it

necessary to include safety instructions on what to do if a customer were to find him or herself in such a bind.

In 2005, the United States Department of Energy safety practices newsletter described the case of a Department of Energy worker who accidentally squirted superglue into his eyes while trying to unclog the tip. This worker was taken by ambulance to the hospital where he spent "several days" waiting for the glue to "work itself loose." The Department of Energy brochure notes that in most cases of superglue misapplication, no "active treatment" is necessary.

Accidental eye gluings happen all the time, largely because the glue bottles resemble eye-drop bottles. It occurs enough that ophthalmologists have been warning their patients (and asking the glue industry to rethink its packaging) for over sixteen years. In 2001, a team of doctors from the Department of Ophthalmology at the Royal Liverpool University Hospital cited a case in which a mother confused antibiotic eye drops prescribed for her baby's conjunctivitis with fingernail adhesive drops. ~~The mother instilled the superglue into the left eye, which caused eyelash clumping, and a slight abrasion to the child's cornea.~~ This same team cited another case in which a three-year-old saw her mother instill medicinal eye drops. Playing "grown-up," the child imitated her mother's actions, using a dropper of superglue instead of eye drops. Both children received emergency medical treatment and were fine. ~~Even still, the incidence of men, women, and children sealing their eyes shut with their "eye drops" would be alarming until a little research revealed that the glue—while certainly inconvenient and uncomfortable—has been shown to cause damage in very, very, very few cases.~~

~~In cases of getting the glue stuck to the inside of your cheek, the "treatment" is simply to let the glue work itself free. Even if the glue were to attach itself directly to the eyeball, according to one brochure, it would detach itself within an hour or to. If you glue your eye or eyes shut, you should flush your eye(s) thoroughly with warm water and cover with a gauze bandage. The glue should work itself out in a few days.~~ The worst harm, it seems, that applying superglue to the human body is that it might burn the skin.

In such cases, the victim is advised to treat the injury like any other burn, after the glue has been removed with warm water. ~~Interestingly, one safety brochure notes that, while it is nearly impossible to swallow superglue (and, thus, poison yourself), it is possible to seal your lips shut! This same brochure notes that it is not likely ever to be necessary to have superglue surgically removed from your body.~~

Exercise 1: Restoring Unity

Each of the following essays and paragraphs lacks unity because of extraneous and superfluous information. For each, identify the sentences (or parts of sentences) that need to be cut to restore unity. Then, explain the edits you made.

1. Passage 1

(1) Bruno Hauptmann, the man accused of kidnapping and murder of famed aviator Charles Lindbergh's infant son, may actually have been guilty of the heinous crime for which he was convicted and executed, but his guilt certainly was not determined by a fair trial at which he was given an adequate defense. (2) Indeed, there was a significant amount of circumstantial evidence and some tentative eyewitness testimony to support the prosecution's claim. (3) Lindbergh testified at the trial that he spoke with a man who called himself "John" to make arrangements to pay ransom for the return of the baby. (4) "John's" voice, according to Lindbergh, sounded very much like Hauptmann's voice. (5) Similarly, John Condon, the family friend chosen to deliver the ransom, testified that the "John" to whom he paid the ransom "resembled" Hauptmann. (6) In fact, Condon's phone number was found written on a closet wall in Hauptmann's kitchen, thus proving that Hauptmann had been in contact with the Lindberghs' friend. (7) After the trial, however, a reporter admitted that *he* had written the phone number in the kitchen closet. (8) Still, there was incriminations evidence against Hauptmann presented at the trial. (9) The Lindbergh baby had been kidnapped from a second-story nursery, and the kidnapper had climbed a ladder to the nursery window. (10) The wood from which the ladder had been made—at least one rail of the ladder (called "rail 16")—matched wood taken from the floor of Bruno Hauptmann's attic perfectly. (11) Both the attic floorboards and "rail 16" even had the identical square nail holes. (12) The fact that the ladder had 400 sets of fingerprints on it, *none* of them belonging to Hauptmann, was not brought up at trial. (13) Neither was the fact that *none* of the footprints or fingerprints collected at the kidnapping scene matched Hauptmann's. (14) The fact remains that $14,000 of ransom money was found in Hauptmann's garage. (15) A movie theater box office attendant testified that Hauptmann had used one of the ransom money's marked bills to purchase a movie ticket. (16) Prosecutors failed to provide the defense with evidence that might have suggested Hauptmann's innocence. (17) Hauptmann himself turned down an offer

of $90,000 from a Hearst newspaper for his public "confession." (18) Still, Bruno Hauptmann was found guilty of the kidnapping and murder and executed in the electric chair, protesting his innocence to the very end.

Sentences and phrases to be cut:

Explanations:

2. Passage 2

(1) The anti-hero of twentieth-century literature is much more than the mere opposite of the traditional, or stereotypical hero of myth, legend, and romance. (2) The modern hero is a complex persona, much more human than a young Wart, who yanks a sword from a rock and is instantly transformed into King Arthur. (3) The popular character of Batman clearly meets the definition of the modern anti-hero.

(4) While the traditional hero seems to be such by birth and destiny, the anti-hero is made by the circumstances of his or her life, typically some secret or tragedy in his past. (5) Thus, the anti-hero is motivated by a negative force like fear or a desire for revenge. (6) Bruce Wayne, Batman's enormously wealthy alter-ego, is haunted by the violent deaths of his parents at the hand of an armed mugger. (7) Young Bruce and his parents were returning home from an evening out when the thug attacked them in a dark alley. (8) The various versions of this initial event play out differently, but one has to wonder why a man as wealthy as the senior Mr. Wayne would have to parade his family through the dark alley rather than having their driver meet them in front of the theater.

(9) Just as the anti-hero has a darker motivation than does the stereotypical hero of olde, the anti-hero is not always a sympathetic or likeable character. (10) King Arthur certainly had his faults, as did Lancelot and Guenivere, but, in the end, he was noble. (11) Not so Bruce Wayne/ Batman. Wayne is a brooding, spoiled-acting playboy, and Batman is an equally brooding night-crawler from whom no child will ever ask an autograph. (12) If one did, Batman would probably snarl at the kid and scare him away. (13) Superman would never do that.

(14) In fact, in the first Superman movie of 1977, we see Superman pause in his night of fighting crime to rescue a kitten from a tree. (15) Now that's what heroes do. (16) Superman is good too, all good. (17) He finds it

nearly impossible to lie, and he does not hurt the criminals he apprehends. (18) Often, he leaves the criminals in comic situations, waiting for the police to arrive and arrest them.

(19) The anti-hero, on the other hand is morally ambiguous, neither good nor bad. (20) Some would say the anti-hero is actually *amoral*, allowing his ends to justify his means. (21) Thus, the anti-hero's actions might be ethically questionable or even potentially illegal. (22) Batman, for example, does work with Commissioner Gordon, but the Caped Crusader does not generally cooperate with the police. (23) He certainly does not worry about due process or civil rights when tracking down his nemeses, and he often resorts to violence. (24) This is especially despicable, given his superior physical conditioning.

(25) Finally, the traditional hero is born or destined for "hero-hood." (26) Arthur was born and raised with magical aid and was the fulfillment of an ancient prophecy. (27) Superman is from another planet. (28) The heroes of Greek and Roman myths and legends were all descended from at least one god. (29) But Batman (Bruce Wayne) is fully human. (30) He is from no supernatural origins and has no super powers. (31) Some might question Batman's status as a superhero, since he is not really "super," but no one can question the fact that he is a perfect example of the twentieth-century anti-hero.

Sentences and phrases to be cut:

Explanations:

3. Passage 3

(1) It's not the biggest comet ever to be seen from Earth. (2) It's not the brightest. (3) It's not even the only comet to return for periodic visits. (4) But Halley's Comet, officially known as 1P/Halley or Comet Halley, is certainly the most famous. (5) Much of the comet's fame originates from its regularity. (6) As astronomer Edmund Halley, for whom the comet is named, calculated, Halley's comet appears in the sky every 75-76 years. (7) It last appeared in 1986, and is scheduled to return in 2061.

(8) While most earthlings have the notion that comets are somewhat akin to shooting stars, glowing and hot, speeding through the Universe, comets really are little more than large chunks of ice and rock—almost like

dirty snowballs in space. (9) Scientists are still trying to discover whether a comet's nucleus is hard like ice or soft and breakable like a snow cone. (10) Either way, the comet's "glow" is reflected sunlight, just like the moon's, and its tail is nothing more than steam and other vapors that trail off the melting and evaporating ice-chunk, as it hurtles closer and closer to the sun.

(11) Most scientists agree that the extinction of the dinosaurs was probably caused when either a comet or an asteroid collided with Earth near what is now the Yucatan Peninsula in Mexico. (12) The nucleus of Halley's comet is approximately 10 miles long, five miles wide, and five miles deep. (13) After the comet's 1986 appearance, novelists Gregory Benford and David Brin wrote *Heart of the Comet*, in which a team of scientists colonizes Halley's comet and builds a settlement deep within the icy nucleus.

(14) Halley's Comet's popularity is also partly due to its regular appearances and its alleged impact on human history. (15) Probably its most famous appearance was in 1066, when it was seen right before the Norman invasion of England. (16) King Harold of England—who had been king only a few months—believed the comet to be an evil omen, and he turned out to be right, as William of Normandy conquered England and became king at the Battle of Hastings. (17) Other appearances of the comet are similarly notable. (18) The recorded appearance of Halley's comet in 12 B.C.E., has led some to speculate that it was the Star of Bethlehem that signaled Jesus' birth in the Gospel of Matthew. (19) Certainly, its appearance in 1301 inspired artist Giotto di Bondone to paint a mural of the Nativity and depict the Star as a glowing, orange comet. (20) A 1986 space probe sent to study Halley's comet as it approached its perihelion—the part of its orbit when it is closest to the sun—was named the Giotto space probe in honor of the famous artist. (21) Two other remarkable appearances of the comet were in 1835 and 1910—the same years as Mark Twain's birth and death. (22) The year before he died, Twain wrote, "I came in with Halley's Comet in 1835. It is coming again next year, and I expect to go out with it." (23) Ironically, he did.

(24) In 1910, the earth actually passed through Comet Halley's gaseous tail. (25) This caused an uproar of panic as the world's press—ignoring the protests of scientists who knew the truth—warned everyone that the comet's poisonous cyanide gas would cause massive deaths. (26) Of course, this did not happen.

(27) Halley's comet was the first comet recognized as returning in regular periods. (28) Once Edmund Halley calculated its orbit, he was not only able to predict when the comet would be returning, but he was also able to examine historical records for times when the comet had already paid us visits. (29) Comets do not have regular orbits the way planets do because

they often come close enough to planets for the planet's gravitational pulls to interfere with the comet's orbit. (30) This is called "orbital perturbation." (31) Dozens of comets orbit the sun and make periodic appearances in our nighttime skies, but none is as anticipated and beloved as 1P/Halley, Halley's Comet.

Sentences and phrases to be cut:

Explanations:

Remember:

Unity has to do with limiting the information you include in a paragraph, essay, or paper so that you stick to your topic.

Coherence is the characteristic that helps your reader follow your train of thought by making it clear *how* the information you present contributes to the point you are trying to establish.

Exercise 2: Revising for Coherence

The following extended essay is very informative and appropriately documented. It is hard to follow, however, because the writer has not paid attention to those aspects of word choice and sentence structure that contribute to a coherent paper.

Rewrite the essay, adding any necessary transitional elements and revising any sentences that do not make clear the relationship between the pieces of information provided.

After you are done, explain why you made the changes you did.

Washington Irving, American author, short story writer, essayist, and poet, is today regarded as the Father of the American short story. Although he is best known today simply as the writer of two classic short stories, as the first American to make a living solely from his writing, he is an essential figure in the development of an American culture—at least an American literary culture.

Irving was born in New York City in 1783. He was the youngest of eleven children. He was also the son of a wealthy merchant. His mother was the English granddaughter of a clergyman. He developed a passion for reading stories about voyages and adventures. *Robinson Crusoe* and the stories of Sinbad, the sailor, were among his favorites. Irving would grow up to become a world traveler. He would earn no small part of his income from his travel writing.

Irving studied law, but never showed too much interest in practicing. He was admitted to the New York bar in 1806, but had already begun to develop a career as a writer, writing for journals and newspapers (Scott 233). He also began his travels, touring Europe from 1804 to 1806. On this trip, he visited Marseilles, Genoa, Sicily, and Rome. He experienced a personal tragedy. This tragedy would have an impact on the rest of his life. He'd earlier become engaged to Matilda Hoffman. She died suddenly, at the age of seventeen, in 1809. The heartbroken Irving would never marry. Years later he wrote to a friend that he dreamed of his "beloved Matilda" every night (Amyliss 17).

Irving was already beginning to build a career and reputation as a writer. His first major work, *A History of New York*, by the imaginary "Dietrich Knickerbocker" (1809) was amazingly popular. The work was about an American city. It was written by an American author. In his award-winning biography of Washington Irving, Josias Scott notes that this *History of New York* would become so influential that "Knickerbocker" would later be used to identify the first American school of writers (154). This school of writers was called the *Knickerbocker Group* (154). Also, any New Yorker who could trace his or her ancestry to original Dutch settlers came to be called a "Knickerbocker" (155). Finally the *Knicks*, the name of the New York City basketball team, is actually short for *Knickerbockers* (155). Not many people know this today.

Irving was a popular writer writing pseudo-historical works. *The Official Washington Irving Fan Club Web Page* explains that he also contributed to the literary notion of the "Noble Savage." This was the idea that—in their primitive innocence—"uncivilized" Native Americans possessed a human integrity far superior to that of the European settlers and their descendents. This was most apparent in Chapter 5 of *A History of New-York from the Beginning of the World to the End of the Dutch Dynasty*, by Dietrich Knickerbocker (1809). It was also apparent in Irving's 1820 essay, "Traits of Indian Character."

The twenty-nine-year-old Irving was appointed military aide to the governor of New York. This was during the War of 1812. He also served as an editor of the *Analetic* magazine in Philadelphia and New York. Irving again left America for Europe. This time he stayed for seventeen years. He lived with his sister and her family in Birmingham, England. He helped with the family hardware business. The business failed, however, and he still stayed in Europe. He wrote *The Sketch Book of Geoffrey Crayon* (Amyliss 334).

"Geoffrey Crayon" was the first-ever portrayal of an American in Europe. Geoffrey Crayon would become Irving's most-used pseudonym. The *Sketch Book* was a collection of stories. This collection sold enough copies, and it earned enough money, that it allowed Irving to become a full-time writer (Scott 546).

Many of Irving's stories were heavily influenced by German folktales. As Nora Amyliss explains, "The Legend of Sleepy Hollow" combines ideas found in numerous tales about supernatural chases. The headless horseman was said to be the decapitated ghost of a Hessian (German) mercenary. Scholars speculate that Irving's famous story is derived from a story by the German academic writer Karl Musäus (89). Musäus was one of the first scholars to collect German folktales and write them down. The more-famous Grimm Brothers were doing the same thing at roughly the same time. In recent years, the Grimms have been accused of plagiarism since they were not the creators of the tales they "wrote." They never claimed, however, to be the creators. The story of the sleepy "Rip Van Winkle" was most likely based on a story called "Peter Klaus the Goatherd" by German writer J.C.C. Nachtigal (97). It is also similar to a Grimm Brothers story, "Karl Katz" (97).

In 1822, Irving was staying in Dresden, Germany. He wrote his sequel to *The Sketch Book of Geoffrey Crayon, Bracebridge Hall*. In 1822 and 1823, Irving was in Dresden. He returned to London in 1824. He stayed in Paris in 1825. He toured Spain from 1826—1831. He returned to England in 1832. He wrote *Columbus, Conquest of Granada*, and *The Companions of Columbus*. This was in Spain. He was so famous as a writer that he was elected to the *Real Academia de la Historia* in 1828 (*Official Washington Irving Fan Club Web Page*). This was also while he was in Spain.

Irving returned to London. He wrote *Alhambra* (Scott 670). He is rumored to have had a romantic relationship with Mary Shelley (Amyliss 429). She was the famous author of *Frankenstein,* It's funny to note that Mary Shelley and her late husband were romantic writers. The term "romantic," has nothing to do with love. Mary's husband's name was Percy. Romantic meant idealistic. But writers who say that Irving and Shelley had a romantic relationship, do mean "love affair." "Romantic" is an ambiguous word.

Irving returned to New York in 1832. He was welcomed as the first American author to achieve international fame (*Official Washington Irving Fan Club Web Page*). American literature was considered second-rate. The only reason an American author would travel to Europe was to "learn how" to create literature.

Irving toured the southern and western states. He wrote *The Crayon Miscellany* and *A Tour of the Prairies* (Scott 700). He finally retired to his house. The house was in the town of Tarrytown-on-Hudson in New York State. It was named Sunnyside. He lived quietly. His brother and sister-in-law lived with him. So did his five nieces (Amyliss 456). It was a period of relative retirement. Irving was visited by Charles Dickens. Dickens and Irving had been longtime pen-pals.

He once again left his beloved Sunnyside. This was 1842. It would be his last trip abroad. Irving was going to serve as the United States Ambassador in Spain. He served as the president of Astor Library. The Astor Library would become the New York Public Library (Scott 753). He also wrote *Mahomet and his Successors.* This book was about the little-understood religion of Islam. He also wrote *Wolfert's Roost,* and his famous five-volume, *The Life of George Washington* (Amyliss 450).

Irving spent the last years of his life in Tarrytown. He died on November 28, 1859. America lost its best-known literary icon. America gained the beginning of a cultural tradition. This tradition is still strong today.

Revision:

Explanation:

Exercise 3: Determining Modes of Development to Meet Certain Rhetorical Purposes

One of the problems inherent in being asked to write a descriptive paragraph or a process analysis is that, as writer, you aren't being told *why* you are writing the description or analysis. When you set out to write to persuade a voter to vote for one candidate instead of another, you suddenly have a reason motivating your description of that person or your analysis of the candidate's political record.

Remember that the most common modes of development are argumentation, analysis, classification, comparison, definition, description, narration, and process.

Following is a list of typical essay topics, writing assignments, and other occasions that might require you to write. List the various modes of development you might need to use in order to achieve that purpose.

For example:

To *persuade* your reader to revise the school cafeteria's menu to reflect more healthful nutrition choices:

- *description* of the current menu
- *description* of typical school lunch
- *description* (and *analysis*) of statistics regarding number of students on free and reduced-fee lunches who have no choice but to eat cafeteria meals
- *analysis* of caloric content, fat content, etc., of a typical school lunch
- *analysis* of nutritionist-recommendations for healthful meals
- *analysis* of cost to produce typical school lunch
- *analysis* of cost to produce healthful lunch
- *process description* of how to enact school- or district-level policy change
- *comparison* of costs of "healthful" versus "typical" meal

1. To *inform* your reader about the connection between litigation and medical expenses

2. To *inform* your reader of the impact of global warming on weather patterns

3. To *inform* your reader about the career of your favorite performer

4. To *inform* your reader about a recent Supreme Court decision

5. To *persuade* your reader to oppose legislation that raises the age to get a driver's license

6. To *persuade* your reader to volunteer for a local Adopt-a-Highway program

7. To *persuade* your reader to participate in a charity walk-a-thon

8. To *persuade* your reader to skip snacks for a week and donate the money to a local food pantry

9. To *persuade* your reader that a recent proposal for a new housing development is not a good idea

10. To *express a personal view* about a new town ordinance

11. To *express a personal view* about your favorite hobby or leisure activity

12. To *express a personal view* about the selection of movies offered by your local theater

13. To *express a personal view* explaining your choice of future career

14. To *express a personal view* about the latest fashion trend among people your age

Exercise 4: Rhetorical Mode, Purpose, and the Research/Extended Essay Topic

Following are some of the research topic-ideas mentioned in Trait One. Each one suggests a number of different approaches to satisfy different purposes. List which modes of development would be most effective in attaining your purpose, and explain why.

As these are all research paper or extended essay topics, you should assume your audience to be your teacher, professor, or an academic committee.

For example:

Sources of...
The Clutter Family killings and Truman Capote's *In Cold Blood* as America's first piece of "journalistic fiction"

to inform the reader of where Capote collected material for his work
- *description of the various sources and the information Capote got from each*
- *narration of Capote's relationship with the killers and how it developed*
- *definition of key terms used within the sources*
- *definition of what you are counting as a source" in your paper*

to persuade the reader that, in addition to his interviews with the killers, A, B, and C were also sources for In Cold Blood
- *description of the various witnesses, newspaper accounts, investigators, etc., and the information (or viewpoints) Capote probably got from each*
- *narration of Capote's interviews with witnesses and others involved in the crime and how he developed his relationships with these sources*
- *definition of key terms used within the sources and the role each source played in the crime or the investigation*
- *definition of what you are counting as a source in your paper*

> • *argumentation to show and discuss evidence which claims that sources are indeed sources*
>
> *to persuade the reader, by establishing what the sources were and then examining the source material, that Y is really nonfiction and should not be considered a novel (or vice-versa)*
>
> > • *description of the various witnesses, newspaper accounts, investigators, etc. and the information (or viewpoints) Capote probably got from each*
> >
> > • *narration of Capote's interviews with witnesses and others involved in the crime and how he developed his relationships with these sources*
> >
> > • *definition of key terms used within the sources and the role each source played in the crime or the investigation*
> >
> > • *definition of what you are counting as a "source" in your paper*
> >
> > • *comparison of source material with the novel itself*
> >
> > • *argumentation to show and discuss that the novel is more a journalistic report of the case than a novel (or vice versa)*

1. Influences on...
  - to *inform* the reader of what Y's influences most likely were

  - to *persuade* the reader that X did indeed influence Y

  - to *persuade* the reader that, contrary to common belief, X did *not* really influence Y

2. Inspirations for...
  - to *inform* the reader of events or people from the author's life, history, etc., that may have inspired events and/or characters in a work

  - to *persuade* the reader that certain events or people did indeed serve as inspirations for...

3. Political, social, cultural contexts of...
  - to *inform* the reader of...

4. Impact of …
- to *inform* the reader of...

- to *persuade* the reader that, contrary to conventional wisdom, X, Y, and Z really are effects of A

5. Causes of …
- to *inform* the reader of...

- to *persuade* the reader that, contrary to conventional wisdom, X, Y, and Z really are causes of A

6. Events leading to…
- to *inform* the reader of...

7. Factors contributing to…
- to *inform* the reader of...

Writing Opportunity: *The College Application Essay*

Towards the last page of just about every one of your college applications is a mostly-blank page with instructions asking you to write a personal essay explaining who you are.

"Personal Essay: This is your opportunity to tell us something about yourself beyond what we can learn from your transcript and résumé," or words to that effect. This indicates who you are beyond a transcript and test scores.

Sometimes a topic will actually be suggested, "Indicate a person, accomplishment, or topical issue that is significant to you, and discuss its significance."

In any event, the college application essay, or personal statement, is the only place in the entire application packet where the members of the admissions committee will be able to hear your voice and meet you as a person.

It is, quite possibly, the most important writing you will have done so far in your life.

Step 1: *Analyze the actual wording of the prompt*

Pay special attention to the verb that you are requested to perform. Are you being asked to *describe,* to *evaluate,* to *narrate,* to *indicate...?*

If you are not *absolutely certain exactly* what the prompt is asking you to write, check the verb's definition in the dictionary, or ask your teacher to help you understand *exactly* what you are being asked to write.

For example: A very common application essay prompt asks you to *indicate* a significant person and to *describe the impact* that person has had on your life. The pitfall here is that the vast majority of applicants choose to respond to this prompt with a character study of the significant person. This is not what has been assigned, and the writer has placed himself or herself at a disadvantage.

Step 2: *Choose your topic*

By now you know how important topic selection is, but in this instance, it is probably even more important because the topic not only establishes the foundation of your paper, but it also becomes the first impression you give the admissions committee of yourself as a person. What you have chosen to write about speaks volumes even before your reader discovers how well you wrote about it.

Here are some crucial do's and don'ts regarding topic choice. All of these suggestions come from college admissions officials themselves, who cite some topics as so popular as to become clichés. Other topics tend to be too difficult to address well, and still others are simply inappropriate topics—things you simply should not share with a committee of total strangers.

Topic Selection Do's and Don't's

DO	DON'T
Do choose a topic that is important to you.	**Don't** choose a topic because you think it will impress the committee.
Do identify the *essential you.*	**Don't** merely rehash what might be inferred from the rest of your application.
Do think in terms of thesis and support.	**Don't** ignore the question and answer your own version of it.
Do answer the question being asked.	**Don't** write a general, one-size-fits-all essay for use on multiple applications.
Do address all variations of the specific question in the specific application.	**Don't** begin to write about the first idea that pops into your head and risk not developing a much better idea that might come later.
Do consider as many topics and approaches as you can.	**Don't** fall into the trap of believing that a vague prompt invites a vague topic.

Warning: Two of the all-time most popular general topics that every admissions officer warns against are what is commonly called the "jock essay" and the "travelogue." This does not mean that—if your participation in sports or your world travels are indeed what you *must* write about to communicate your essential self—you can't write about them. It does, however, mean that you should know from the very beginning that you will be including yourself in a huge stack of essays on a similar topic and you must develop the unique *youness* of the topic in order to be successful.

Time Clue: Even if you are a terrible procrastinator, you should actually allow yourself several weeks to think about—and jot down—various potential topics.

Step 3: *Choose an approach and organizational plan*

Again, you need to look closely at what *exactly* you are being asked to do in this essay. To be asked to *indicate* a significant person and to describe the *influence* is not an invitation to describe the person.

To *evaluate* an experience like a winning game or a trip to Europe is not the same as *describing* or *narrating* step-by-step and blow-by-blow the individual steps and events of the experience.

Step 4: *Draft your theses*

Theses is the plural for thesis. Just as you brainstormed a number of different potential topics and experimented with a number of different organization plans and approaches, you'll want to try out a number of different theses.

Again, however, make certain your thesis addresses the prompt and does not send you off on a tangent.

Compare:

> My sophomore English teacher, Mrs. Frances McFarland, has been one of the most significant people in my life so far.

with:

> Had I not had Mrs. Frances McFarland for English in my sophomore year, I would probably never have dared to take the most challenging junior and senior courses, and would never have presumed to apply for a college the caliber of _____.

The first one is so vague, it says essentially nothing about your teacher, Mrs. McFarland, or the influence she had on you. It could also very easily lead to a description of Mrs. McFarland, when the admissions committee wants to read about *you.*

The second specifies the influence Mrs. McFarland had on you, and focuses immediately on those details that will explain your apparent journey from uncertain underachiever to someone finally recognizing his or her full potential.

This is what the admissions committee wants to read.

>
> **Time Clue:** Again, you can give yourself a week or so to think and try out a number of different approaches—for a number of different potential topics. This is an important essay, so you do not want the absence of a firm deadline to lull you into believing you don't need to be working toward your final essay.

Step 5: *Brainstorm more support for each thesis*

This step should also include eliminating those details that don't *directly* address the point the prompt is asking you to make.

Step 6: *Draft your outlines*

Due to the predictable nature of some of the biggest potential pitfalls for this essay, it is essential to draft as full and complete an outline as possible for *each* of your theses.

Step 7: *Set your outlines aside for a day or two*

Give them to people you trust to look at and comment on. Ask them to make certain that *you* are at the center of each of the discussions and that each of the discussions actually addresses the prompt.

Step 8: *Look at your own outlines with a fresh and critical eye*

Ask yourself the same things you asked your friends above. Be your own worst critic.

>
> **Time Clue:** This portion should take a couple of days, maybe a week. You should be working on your college application essays a little bit each day.

Step 9: *Write your first draft(s)*

Choose what you consider to be (and what others have told you is) your strongest thesis and outline.

Or, go ahead and write the drafts of a few of your essays.

> **Time Clue:** Because of your work in Steps 1–8, you are well prepared to write. This draft should take only an hour or so to compose. If you find yourself struggling to "come up with" ideas, stop and choose another of your theses and outlines to develop.

Step 10: *Put your first draft aside for two days*

As always, this is a very important step. You want to allow time to pass between writing your draft and rereading it for revision. This makes it easier for you to notice errors, correct them, and have a more powerful essay.

During these couple of days, show your draft to the people who looked at and commented on your outline to make certain you are delivering what the outline promised. You should also show it to a few people who didn't look at your outline, so that they can look at it with fresh eyes and tell you whether you are addressing the requirements of the prompt.

Step 11: *Write your final draft*

Step 12: *Attach your essay to your application and send it.*

Trait Three
Sentence Structure and Variety

Determining the Readability of Your Writing

In addition to helping to establish tone and voice and clarifying relative importance of the information you are conveying, the length and structure of the sentences you compose help to determine the readability of your writing. Basically, an essay or paper's readability is a measure of how difficult or easy it is to read. Another way of looking at it would be to say it is a measure of how many years of school a reader would need in order to understand your essay. You don't really need to begin performing a readability study on everything you write, but it is important for you to be aware of the issue.

Make Yours Better!

Indian music is a very different system from European music. One of the main differences is the *raga*. What exactly is a *raga* is difficult for many newcomers to Indian music to understand. Probably the best explanation is that it is a very complex set of rules for how to play certain music to evoke a certain "color" or mood in the listener. In fact, that is what the word *raga* means: a color.

Musicians can choose a *raga* for a particular time of day, season of the year, special festival, or other occasion. For example, at the time of the year of seasonal rains, there are special *ragas*. Sometimes, however, even though a *raga* is supposed to be used for a particular time of day, it is impossible for the musicians to play then or for the audience to attend; in these circumstances, the most important thing is that the music brings out a certain feeling in the audience.

A *raga* is not one particular song, scale, note, or rhythm. It is something related to all of these things. For example, one aspect of the *raga* is the *swara*, or notes. There are seven *swara*. They each have a long form and an abbreviated form: *shadj (sa), risabh (re), gandhara (ga), madhyam (ma), pancham (pa), dhaivat (dha), and nishad (ni)*. The group of the notes together is called the *sargam (sa, re, ga, ma)*, just as the eight notes in Western music *(do, re, mi, fa, so, la, ti, do)* are collectively

> Notice the varied sentence structure in this paragraph. The author mixes in different kinds of sentences so that the language sounds natural, not awkward.

> Each paragraph begins with a different kind of sentence so that the language does not become repetitive or boring.

called an *octave*. The system of assigning syllable names to musical tones (*do* and *dhaivat*) is called *solfege*.

Another aspect is the *that* of the *raga*, which shows the musician which group of notes to use. A *that* is more like a mode in Western music than a scale, because—while a scale is a group of notes—a mode is a group of notes that starts and ends on a particular note. The *that*, like the mode, has to start and end on a certain *swara*. Each *that* is a different interpretation of the seven *swara*, but one thing that never changes is that the first and fifth *swara* are always *sa* and *pancham* respectively.

How, do Indian musicians create a particular mood or tone for their listeners? Much depends on the *jati*, the number of notes in a particular *raga*. The *jati* may use five, six, or all seven *swara*. Or the *raga* might require a mixed *jati*, which would mean it used a different number of notes ascending and descending the *sargam*. Ascending and descending the *sargam* are called *avarohana* and *arohana* respectively. Even these have special twists and turns called the *vakra*.

Clearly, there are many different, special rules for playing Indian music according to the *raga*. It is very different from Western music, and might take a Western musician a long while to learn to appreciate its beauty and complexity.

> ▧ Asking and answering questions can be another way to vary the sentence structure and keep the passage interesting.

Essay Critique

The author of this passage includes a lot of appropriate and interesting information about ragas. He or she presents this information in a way that keeps the reader engaged; the sentences are both long and short and come in the form of both statements and questions, just as in a conversation or lecture.

This essay receives a score of 10 on the:

Sentence Structure Rubric

14 = ACCOMPLISHED
The **writer's sentence** formation choices reflect a thorough understanding of the topic and how best to communicate it to meet the needs of the audience and the purpose of the writing.

13 = **Variety in sentence** structure and length generally contributes to the overall impact of the essay, but opportunities to communicate more clearly or to enliven the essay with sentence variety are sometimes missed.

12 = **Variety in sentence** structure and length enhances the overall clarity and impact of the essay.

11 = **Variety in sentence** structure and length is used to strengthen the impact of the essay.

10 = PROFICIENT
Sentence formation is adequate to meet the needs of the subject, audience, and purpose.

Readability and Sentence Length and Structure

There is absolutely nothing grammatically, syntactically, or rhetorically wrong with the following sentences. In fact, their combination of main and subordinate clauses, modified by their numerous noun, verb, and prepositional phrases, allows them both to communicate some fairly complex ideas. However, their length and complexity do make them difficult to follow.

> Let the word go forth from this time and place, to friend and foe alike, that the torch has been passed to a new generation of Americans—born in this century, tempered by war, disciplined by a hard and bitter peace, proud of our ancient heritage—and unwilling to witness or permit the slow undoing of those human rights to which this Nation has always been committed, and to which we are committed today at home and around the world.

> To those peoples in the huts and villages across the globe struggling to break the bonds of mass misery, we pledge our best efforts to help them help themselves, for whatever period is required—not because the Communists may be doing it, not because we seek their votes, but because it is right.

> Inaugural Address of President John F. Kennedy
> January 20, 1961

Notice how the long, complicated sentences, when broken into a number of shorter and simpler sentences, are somewhat easier to follow—even if some of the beauty of the language is also lost in the translation:

> Let the word go forth from this time and place, to friend and foe alike.
> The torch has been passed to a new generation of Americans.
> These new Americans were born in this century.
> We have been tempered by war.
> We have been disciplined by a hard and bitter peace.
> We are proud of our ancient heritage.
> We are unwilling to witness or permit the slow undoing of human rights.
> This Nation has always been committed to those rights.
> We are committed to them today at home and around the world.

> To those peoples in the huts and villages across the globe struggling to break the bonds of mass misery, we pledge our best efforts.
> We will help them help themselves.
> We will help them for whatever period is required.
> We'll do it, not because the Communists may be doing it.
> We'll do it, not because we seek their votes.
> We'll do it because it is right.

Exercise 1: Clarifying Lengthy Sentences

Rewrite each of the following sentences to break them into a number of shorter, simpler sentences. Then, explain the impact—both positive and negative—your changes have on both the readability and eloquence of the original.

For example:

We hold these truths to be self-evident: that all men are created equal, that they are endowed by their Creator with certain unalienable Rights, that among these are Life, Liberty and the pursuit of Happiness, that to secure these rights, Governments are instituted among Men—deriving their just powers from the consent of the governed, —that whenever any Form of Government becomes destructive of these ends, it is the Right of the People to alter or to abolish it, and to institute new Government, laying its foundation on such principles and organizing its powers in such form, as to them shall seem most likely to effect their Safety and Happiness.

- United States Declaration of Independence
July 4, 1776

Revision: *It goes without saying that all men are created equal and that they are endowed by their Creator with certain unalienable rights. We further believe it to be beyond discussion that Life, Liberty, and the pursuit of Happiness are three of those rights. Finally, it is apparent to us that Governments are instituted for the sole purpose of securing these rights, and that a true Government has only as much power as the people allow it to have. Should any Government begin to destroy the rights it was instituted to protect, it is the people's right to alter it or to abolish it outright and institute a new government—one which they can agree is best able to protect their God-given and unalienable rights.*

Explanation: *While the rhetorical effect of the parallel constructions ("that all men..." "that they are endowed..." "that among..." "that to secure..." etc.) is lost, the concept of an "unalienable right" and what is a "self-evident truth" is made clearer.*

1. We shall defend our island, whatever the cost may be, we shall fight on the beaches, we shall fight on the landing grounds, we shall fight in the fields and in the streets, we shall fight in the hills; we shall never surrender.

–Winston Churchill

Revision:

Explanation:

2. Here before me is the Bible used in the inauguration of our first President, in 1789, and I have just taken the oath of office on the Bible my mother gave me a few years ago, opened to a timeless admonition from the ancient prophet Micah:

"He hath showed thee, O man, what is good; and what doth the Lord require of thee, but to do justly, and to love mercy, and to walk humbly with thy God." (Micah 6:8)

–Inaugural Address of President Jimmy Carter
January 20, 1977

Revision:

Explanation:

3. Aim at perfection in everything, though in most things it is unattainable. However, they who aim at it, and persevere, will come much nearer to it than those whose laziness and despondency make them give it up as unattainable.

–Lord Chesterfield

Revision:

Explanation:

4. Yet each man kills the thing he loves, by each let this be heard, some do it
   with a bitter look, some with a flattering word. The coward does it with a
   kiss, the brave man with a sword!

   –Oscar Wilde

Revision:

Explanation:

5. A monarchy is the most expensive of all forms of government, the regal state
   requiring a costly parade, and he who depends on his own power to rule,
   must strengthen that power by bribing the active and enterprising whom he
   cannot intimidate.

   –James F. Cooper

Revision:

Explanation:

6. Wit is so shining a quality that everybody admires it; most people aim at it,
   all people fear it, and few love it unless in themselves. A man must have a
   good share of wit himself to endure a great share of it in another.

   –Lord Chesterfield

Revision:

Explanation:

7. Our ambition should be to rule ourselves, the true kingdom for each one of us; and true progress is to know more, and be more, and to do more.

–Oscar Wilde

Revision:

Explanation:

8. In war as in life, it is often necessary when some cherished scheme has failed, to take up the best alternative open, and if so, it is folly not to work for it with all your might.

–Winston Churchill

Revision:

Explanation:

9. Its failings notwithstanding, there is much to be said in favor of journalism in that by giving us the opinion of the uneducated, it keeps us in touch with the ignorance of the community.

–Oscar Wilde

Revision:

Explanation:

10. Horse-play, romping, frequent and loud fits of laughter, jokes, and indiscriminate familiarity, will sink both merit and knowledge into a degree of contempt. They compose at most a merry fellow; and a merry fellow was never yet a respectable man.

–Lord Chesterfield

Revision:

Explanation:

Cohesion and Readability

While almost all of the most commonly used readability measures take the length of the sentences (words per sentence) into account, almost none look at the structure of the sentence. A few, however, take into consideration the *cohesion*[1] (the logical connection and progression of ideas) of information in two or more consecutive sentences.

Consider the following two passages. Both Flesch Reading Ease[2] scores are in the "easy" range, but notice how the "low cohesion" of the first set of sentences makes it more difficult to read:

Low Cohesion: Donna's dog broke its leash. The cat ran into the street. Muriel slammed on her brakes. The milk spilled.

High Cohesion: Because the cat ran into the street when Donna's dog broke its leash, Muriel slammed on her brakes and spilled the milk.

---

[1]In the previous Trait, we discussed the *coherence* of the essay. *Cohesion* is a part of coherence. It is important that you do not confuse the two.

[2]The Flesch Reading Ease scale will be defined and discussed in greater detail in Trait 6.

Exercise 2: Explaining the Role of Cohesion in Ease of Reading

In each of the following sets, the "high cohesion" sentence is actually easier to read, even if it might have a lower score on the Flesch Reading Ease scale. Explain how the combined sentences and the use of subordinating and coordinating conjunctions assist the reader, even if they make for longer, more complex sentences.

For example:

Low Cohesion: Jeremy Reynolds is an extremely bright child. He wants to be a lawyer. He wants to be a Supreme Court Justice.

High Cohesion: Jeremy Reynolds is an extremely bright child, who wants to be not just a lawyer, but also a Supreme Court Justice.

Explanation: *The three simple sentences in the "low cohesion" version imply that the three bits of information—Jeremy is bright, he wants to be a lawyer, and he wants to be a Supreme Court Justice—are all equally important. There is no single main idea that the other ideas support. The "high cohesion" version makes it clear that the main idea is that Jeremy is bright. Second in importance is that he wants to be a Supreme Court Justice. The contrast between not just a lawyer but also a Supreme Court Justice is much clearer in this example.*

1. LOW COHESION: The Nabateans used Aramaic heavily in their inscriptions. Their names are in Arabic. Their everyday speech was probably also in Arabic.

HIGH COHESION: The Nabateans used Aramaic heavily in their inscriptions, but their names are in Arabic; and so, probably, was their everyday speech.

Explanation:

2. LOW COHESION: They settled between the Dead Sea and the Red Sea. The land they occupied had once been called Edom.

HIGH COHESION: They settled between the Dead Sea and the Red Sea, in the land that had once been called Edom.

Explanation:

3. LOW COHESION: Wealthy Greeks and Romans wanted frankincense and myrrh. They liked to perfume their homes. The processes of daily life filled their homes with foul odors. The frankincense and myrrh helped to mask these odors. These spices came from the southern end of Arabia. This is the area of a modern-day nation called Yemen. This area was called "Happy Arabia" in Greek and Latin.

HIGH COHESION: Wealthy Greeks and Romans wanted frankincense and myrrh to perfume their homes and mask the foul odors of daily life. These spices came from the southern end of Arabia—modern-day Yemen—which was called "Happy Arabia" in Greek and Latin.

Explanation:

4. LOW COHESION: Gaza was the nearest Mediterranean port to "Happy Arabia." It was almost 2,000 miles away from "Happy Arabia." The land between Gaza and "Happy Arabia" was all desert.

HIGH COHESION: Between "Happy Arabia" and Gaza, which was the nearest port on the Mediterranean coast, lay almost 2,000 miles of desert.

Explanation:

5. LOW COHESION: The Nabateans occupied the land. The Nabateans had camels. Camels could travel the desert while carrying heavy burdens. The Nabateans knew how to collect water from winter rains and store it in secret cisterns.

HIGH COHESION: The Nabateans, who occupied this land, knew how to collect water from winter rains to store in secret cisterns, and used camels to carry heavy loads through the desert.

Explanation:

6. LOW COHESION: In Rome, a pound of top-quality incense would cost 6 denarii. This was more than two weeks' wages for the average Roman. Camels can comfortably carry about 330 pounds. The incense carried by a single camel would have brought in about 2000 denarii. Much of this money went to the Nabateans.

HIGH COHESION: In Rome, a pound of top-quality incense would cost 6 denarii, which was more than two weeks' wages for the average Roman. Since camels can comfortably carry about 330 pounds, the incense carried by a single camel would have brought in about 2000 denarii, much of which went to the Nabateans.

Explanation:

7. LOW COHESION: The Nabateans established themselves as an important transporter of precious goods. In the 2nd century B.C.E., they conquered the Red Sea coast south to Happy Arabia. They took over the Indian trade. This included cinnamon. They added the silk trade. The silk trade originated in China.

HIGH COHESION: The Nabateans thus established themselves as an important transporter of precious goods. In the 2nd century B.C.E., they conquered the Red Sea coast south to "Happy Arabia," where they took over the Indian trade, including cinnamon. Later, they added the silk trade from China.

Explanation:

8. LOW COHESION: The capital of the Nabataean empire was a city called Petra. It was carved entirely out of sandstone cliffs. It was located in a part of the desert that is now Jordan.

HIGH COHESION: The capital of the Nabatean empire was a city, carved entirely out of sandstone cliffs in the desert of what is now modern-day Jordan, called Petra.

Explanation:

9. LOW COHESION: The early Nabataeans disliked houses. They feared that they would be conquered by a more powerful people. They feared they would become the slaves of these conquerors. They reasoned that permanent buildings and immobility would cause this.

HIGH COHESION: The early Nabataeans disliked houses, fearing that permanent buildings and immobility would result in their being conquered and enslaved by a more powerful people.

Explanation:

10. LOW COHESION: Still, they gradually gave up their nomadic life. They embraced a more urban existence. They established Petra some time in the third century B.C.E. Historians do not really understand why.

HIGH COHESION: Still, for reasons that historians do not fully understand, they gradually gave up their nomadic life for an urban existence, establishing Petra some time in the third century B.C.E.

Explanation:

Sentence structure and word choice both help you maintain cohesion.

The clock in the tower struck twelve. Cinderella ran to the carriage. She lost her shoe.

When the clock tower struck twelve, Cinderella ran to the carriage and lost her shoe.

Exercise 3: Revising for Cohesion

Each of the following groups of sentences has a high reading ease score, but low cohesion. Rewrite each to increase the cohesion and make the information in the sentences easier to follow.

For example:

Low Cohesion: John Partridge was a shoemaker. He began printing almanacs to make some extra money. He claimed to be able to predict the future. He challenged his readers to submit predictions for the future to him. Jonathan Swift wrote in a prediction that Partridge would die. He used the name Isaac Bickerstaff. Later he wrote in to say that Bickerstaff's prediction had come true. He used a different name. Partridge protested that he was still alive. No one believed him.

Revision: *John Partridge, a shoemaker by trade, began printing almanacs to make some extra money. He claimed to be able to predict the future and invited his readers to submit predictions to him. Jonathan Swift, using the name Isaac Bickerstaff, wrote in a prediction that Partridge would die. Later, using another pseudonym, Swift wrote that Bickerstaff's prediction had come true. Partridge protested that he was very much alive, but no one believed him.*

1. LOW COHESION: *Gulliver's Travels* was published in 1726. This was Swift's first major prose work. It's been considered a children's book since Victorian times. It's really a satire of the politics of the times. Swift also satirizes eighteenth-century science. Most people did not "get" the satire. People do not "get" satire today either.

Revision:

2. LOW COHESION: In 1729, Swift wrote "A Modest Proposal." This is the other of his most famous satires. It is supposedly written by an intelligent and objective Irishman. The proposal addresses how to end poverty and overpopulation in Ireland. The author suggests that the poor should sell their children. These children could be cooked and eaten by rich Englishmen.

Revision:

3. LOW COHESION: Jonathan Swift was born in Dublin, Ireland, on November 30, 1667. His parents were Jonathan Swift and Abigaile Erick Swift. He was their second child. He was also their only son.

Revision:

4. LOW COHESION: Swift's father died seven months before Swift was born. His mother probably returned to England. She left Swift to be raised by his father's family.

Revision:

5. LOW COHESION: Swift worked as a secretary to Sir William Temple. In Sir William's household, he met Esther Johnson. Swift called Esther Johnson "Stella." He became her tutor. Some biographers say he married Stella in 1716. There is no proof of this. They lived near each other for most of their lives. They were always very properly chaperoned. It is possible they were never alone together.

Revision:

6. LOW COHESION: When Swift met Esther Johnson, she was 8 years old. She had no father. She was the daughter of one of Sir William's household servants.

Revision:

7. LOW COHESION: Swift returned to Ireland in 1690. He left Sir William's household because of his health. He returned the following year. Swift was experiencing fits of vertigo or giddiness. The disease he had is now called Ménière's disease. This would plague Swift for his entire life.

Revision:

8. LOW COHESION: Sir William had died in 1699. Many of Sir William's family did not approve of Swift. They also did not like how Swift had edited Sir William's memoirs. Swift decided to approach King William. He believed he had a connection to the king through Sir William. He also believed that he had been promised a position.

Revision:

9. LOW COHESION: Swift became acquainted with the Vanhomrigh family. He became involved with one of the daughters, Hester. Hester also did not have a father. Swift gave Hester the nickname "Vanessa." Their correspondence suggests that Hester was infatuated with Swift. He may have reciprocated her affection. He then probably tried to break it off. Hester followed Swift to Ireland in 1714. There appears to have been a confrontation. Esther Johnson may have been involved.

Revision:

10. LOW COHESION: Swift died on October 19, 1745. He was 78 years old. He had been ill for some time. Many believed he had gone insane. Really, he had a neurological disorder. It was called Ménière's Disease. It was a disorder of the middle ear. Sufferers of Ménière's Disease experience terrible headaches. They also feel dizzy all the time. Swift had been told that the citizens of Dublin wanted to celebrate his birthday. He replied, "It is all folly; they had better leave it alone." This happened two years before Swift died.

Revision:

Exercise 4: Revising for Cohesion

The following paragraph has a fairly high reading ease score, but low cohesion. Revise the paragraph to increase the cohesion and make the author's main idea more apparent and the development easier to follow.

The Grand Canyon in Arizona is often listed as one of the Seven Natural Wonders of the World. Geologists are not absolutely certain of the canyon's origins or age. They agree on its general history and formation. The Grand Canyon is the one of the United States' most wondrous sights. The Grand Canyon is a huge erosion ditch. It has been carved out of the Arizona sandstone by the Colorado River. This has happened over a period of five or six million years. Sandstone is soft. The Colorado River flows fairly rapidly. It flowed even faster during the melting of ice ages and periods of increased precipitation. The Grand Canyon is the result of a combination of these factors. The Grand Canyon is more than a mile deep. That is its deepest measurement. It is 277 miles long. Imagine a stream of water from an open garden hose flowing down a large pile of dirt. The flowing water will cause erosion to the pile. The longer the water flows, the deeper and wider the eroded channel will be. Runoff from rain and snowfall also plays a role. It is hard to imagine. Such a majestic display of colorful rock and fanciful formations could have been carved out by something so apparently innocent as water. There is a lesson to be learned here. The forces of nature still shape the character of the planet. We naively believe we can control it.

Revision:

The art of considering both sides of an argument is called *Dialectical Reasoning*. It is a useful mode of thinking to master for much of the writing you will find yourself doing for the rest of your life.

The basic assumption of *dialectical reasoning* is that in order for a thinker to consider two sides of an argument, the argument must have two sides.

Writing Opportunity: *The Homework Essay: A Dialectic*

The first side is generally called the "thesis." The second side is called the "antithesis."

The middle ground, the new idea that the thinker/writer develops by considering the thesis and antithesis, is the "synthesis."

For example:

Thesis: America's dependence on foreign oil was first caused, and continues to be exacerbated, by the huge multi-national oil corporations whose sole motivation is profit.

Some evidence that might be collected to support this thesis includes:

- the different types of alternative fuel that exist and the length of time they have been available

- data on plant-based fuels like ethanol and how other countries are already successfully marketing these fuels

- evidence to suggest that alternative fuel and automotive technologies might actually have been suppressed.

Antithesis: The passion the American people have for fast cars, bright lights, and an automated life of luxury will continue to perpetuate our dependence on foreign oil, despite private industry innovations and government policies.

Some evidence that might be collected to support this antithesis includes:

- data comparing American energy consumption with that of other industrial nations

- comparison of the typical American home with that of other industrial nations, especially comparing the presence and use of time-saving appliances, lights, electronics, etc.

- any evidence to suggest that when the government has called for voluntary cut-backs in energy consumption, they have been largely ignored

- any evidence of Americans' hesitation to use alternative fuels or transportation technologies.

Synthesis: Convenience and comfort are so embedded in the American consciousness, and the capitalistic passion for profit is so strong, that it is highly unlikely that a satisfactory solution to our dependence on foreign oil will be discovered any time soon.

Step 1: *Choose your topic*

Think of an issue that interests you, but one about which you either have no strong opinion or for which you understand both sides of the argument.

At this stage, it isn't a bad idea to think of three or four issues that might become topics for your dialectic.

Step 2: *Draft your thesis and antithesis*

As in the above example, the thesis and antithesis should represent opposite positions of the issue. For both the thesis and the antithesis, you should have some idea of the types of information you will need to support each view.

Time Clue: Assume you've been given two weeks for this essay. You can take a full day or two for Steps 1 and 2.

Step 3: *Research both your thesis and antithesis*

Just as you did in Trait Four, develop a shopping list of the information you are going to look for, survey the Internet, and visit various libraries to locate the information you need to discuss each view. Look at your sources and take notes.

> **Remember:** Even though your dialectic will present only information *in support* of each view, you should still take notes that contradict each view as well. These will help you arrive at your synthesis. **Also,** do not forget that you will need all three types of notes for your essay: information directly from your sources, your reaction to the sources, and original ideas.

> **Time Clue:** For a two-week essay, you can afford four or five days for the research.

Step 4: *Draft your synthesis*

Examine all of the information you have gathered both in support of and refuting the two sides of your issue. In a single sentence, state the middle ground, the compromise.

This synthesis will ultimately be the thesis statement of your essay. For the sake of clarity, we will also refer to the thesis statement in this assignment as the main idea.

Step 5: *Draft your outline*

Again, think like your intended reader. What is the most logical way to lead your reader to see the validity of your synthesis?

The obvious choices are probably (1) to discuss the thesis, transition into a discussion of the antithesis, and then finally establish your synthesis (main idea), or (2) to alternate between the thesis and antithesis, discussing each point-by-point, finally transitioning to your synthesis (main idea).

Step 6: *Write your first draft*

Step 7: *Revise and rewrite*

Set your draft aside for the night. Then, read it critically and make all necessary revisions.

Before completing your final draft, show your draft to one or two other people and take their comments into consideration.

Step 8: *Your essay is done. Submit it.*

Trait Four

Conventions of
Written English

TRAIT FOUR:
CONVENTIONS OF WRITTEN ENGLISH

Make Yours Better!

For a balloonist, there is only one place to be: the balloon festival that outdoes all the rest. It has beautiful balloons all taking off together, exciting races and competitions, and hundreds of top balloonists trading stories and ballooning tips. This is the International Balloon Fiesta in Albuquerque, New Mexico, which is always held the first week of October.

Albuquerque is considered by many balloonists the best place in the world for ballooning. A very stable wind pattern called the "Albuquerque Box" makes it easy for the pilots to control and land their craft. Basically, because Albuquerque lies along a river, the Rio Grande, and in the Sandia Mountains, there are layers of winds flowing in opposite directions. Balloonists can ride the wind flowing one way, then increase their altitude and ride a higher layer of wind going the other way. This is very useful to competitors at the Balloon Fiesta because it helps them easily launch, control, and land their balloons.

- Proper names are correctly capitalized.

The wind pattern is best for ballooning in the early morning and evening. In the morning, there are amazing mass ascensions, which launch hundreds of balloons at once. First, a balloon flying the American flag is launched while "The Star-Spangled Banner" plays. Then, launch directors guide the other balloons in a two-wave launch. The directors are called "zebras" because they wear black and white stripes. In the evening, spectators can watch one of the glow events, in which balloons light up the night sky with their softly glowing propane jets. A "special-shapes" "glowdeo" launches balloons of unusual shape at night.

- Adverbial phrases telling when and where are set off by commas.

Other events in the Fiesta include the America's Challenge Gas Balloon race and the Fiesta Challenge Competition. The Gas Balloon race starts in Albuquerque, but it ends far away. Gas balloons can stay in the air for up to sixty hours, unlike hot air balloons, which can stay up for only about two hours. The winner of the Gas Balloon challenge is the person who gets the farthest away; it could even be Canada or the East Coast. In the Fiesta Challenge Competition, the goal is to drop a marker closest to a target on the ground.

- A semicolon is used here to set off the first independent clause from a second one that explains it.

Hundreds of thousands of people gather in Albuquerque to watch the Balloon Fiesta. Although it started with thirteen balloons taking off from a shopping center parking lot, it is now one of the biggest balloon events in the world.

Essay Critique

The author of this passage spells and punctuates everything correctly. Because we are not distracted by errors, we can focus on the subject matter of the passage.

This essay receives a score of 10 on the:

Conventions Rubric

14 = ACCOMPLISHED
Language is skillfully used throughout the essay. Sentence structure, punctuation, and artful use of Poetic License contribute significantly to the overall impact of the piece.

13 = Errors resulting from experimentation with form and usage are infrequent and do not interfere with the reader's understanding.

12 = Errors resulting from experimentation with form and usage do not severely interfere with the reader's understanding, but suggest the need for editing and minor revision.

11 = Having gained control over conventions, the writer begins to experiment with new constructions, usages, etc., for effect of communication. This experimentation, however, may result in awkward, incorrect, or inappropriate usage that requires careful editing and some revision to correct.

10 = PROFICIENT
The essay is free of surface errors (grammar, spelling, punctuation, etc.).

Toward More Powerful Language Use

In the previous book, our three simple truths began to overlap, and the focus shifted from an individual study of word choice, sentence structure, and language to a combination of the three. You already know that sometimes you will need to favor correctness over style, while at other times you will want to commit some minor error for the sake of maintaining a tone or voice.

The deciding factor lies in your ability to control every aspect of your language, your word choice, sentence structure, grammar, and mechanics. A "stylish" paper that makes no sense is just as faulty as a fully correct, perfectly clear, but thoroughly dull and lifeless paper. As a proficient writer, you can get away with many unconventional uses as long as you understand:

- what you are doing and why
- why what you are doing is *usually* considered incorrect or inappropriate
- how your reader will react to your creative license.

Using Connotations Powerfully

You already know that the dictionary definition of a word is called its **denotation** while the commonly-accepted understanding of a word's meaning and use is its **connotation.**

A word's **connotation** differs from its **denotation** largely in terms of emotional values. Consider the following list:

> arrange
> plan
> plot
> conspire

On the denotative level, each word means essentially the same thing: to draw or devise a series of actions intended to produce some desired end or result. Yet, on the connotative level, each word takes on an emotional value.

To *arrange* something is generally positive. The series of actions being devised is intended to be pleasant or helpful. We *arrange* parties and receptions. We make *arrangements* to pick someone up at the airport.

Plan does not have the strongly positive connotation of arrange, but it does not have any strong negative connotations, either. It is neutral.

Plot and *conspire*, however, both have negative connotations. *Conspiracy* is, in fact, the charge levied against a person accused of helping another plan to commit a crime.

For example, Britain's Guy Fawkes Day commemorates the failed *plot* to blow up the houses of Parliament, not the failed *arrangements.*

Understanding the connotative, emotional values your reader is likely to attach to a given word is essential for powerful writing. On the one hand, you want to make certain you avoid an unwanted emotional response. On the other hand, you certainly want to use the words you know will move your readers in the way you want them to be moved.

Exercise 1: Assessing the Emotional Connotations of Synonyms

Following is a list of words, each accompanied by one or more words or phrases that are generally synonymous. Indicate whether the word or phrase has a strongly negative, strongly positive, mildly negative, mildly positive, or neutral connotation. Then, use each word in a sentence that indicates the emotional connotation of the word.

For example:

PREVENT

Emotional connotation: *neutral or mildly positive*

Sentence: *While momentarily unpleasant, many injections are given for the purpose of preventing a serious disease.*

DETER

Emotional connotation: *neutral or positive*

Sentence: *Once his mind is set, it is almost impossible to deter Hezekiah from his course of action.*

OBSTRUCT

Emotional connotation: *negative*

Sentence: *Anna-Louise was charged with obstructing justice when she failed to answer all of the questions during the police interview.*

1. <u>REFORM</u>

Emotional connotation:

Sentence:

<u>CHANGE</u>

Emotional connotation:

Sentence:

<u>ADAPT</u>

Emotional connotation:

Sentence:

<u>EVOLVE</u>

Emotional connotation:

Sentence:

<u>DEVELOP</u>

Emotional connotation:

Sentence:

2. <u>PROSPERITY</u>

Emotional connotation:

Sentence:

<u>WEALTH</u>

Emotional connotation:

Sentence:

<u>ABUNDANCE</u>

Emotional connotation:

Sentence:

3. <u>LIBERTY</u>

Emotional connotation:

Sentence:

<u>FREEDOM</u>

Emotional connotation:

Sentence:

<u>LICENSE</u>

Emotional connotation:

Sentence:

4. <u>COMMITMENT</u>

Emotional connotation:

Sentence:

<u>PROMISE</u>

Emotional connotation:

Sentence:

<u>CONTRACT</u>

Emotional connotation:

Sentence:

<u>OBLIGATION</u>

Emotional connotation:

Sentence:

5. DUTY

Emotional connotation:

Sentence:

OBLIGATION

Emotional connotation:

Sentence:

PRIVILEGE

Emotional connotation:

Sentence:

MANDATE

Emotional connotation:

Sentence:

6. PRECIOUS

Emotional connotation:

Sentence:

DEAR

Emotional connotation:

Sentence:

EXPENSIVE

Emotional connotation:

Sentence:

RARE

Emotional connotation:

Sentence:

BELOVED

Emotional connotation:

Sentence:

7. <u>**PREMISE**</u>

Emotional connotation:

Sentence:

<u>**IDEA**</u>

Emotional connotation:

Sentence:

<u>**THESIS**</u>

Emotional connotation:

Sentence:

8. <u>**TOUGH**</u>

Emotional connotation:

Sentence:

<u>**HARD**</u>

Emotional connotation:

Sentence:

<u>**COARSE**</u>

Emotional connotation:

Sentence:

<u>**BRUTAL**</u>

Emotional connotation:

Sentence:

9. **LEAD**

Emotional connotation:

Sentence:

COMMAND

Emotional connotation:

Sentence:

BOSS

Emotional connotation:

Sentence:

Exercise 2: Examining Synonyms and Connotations

Following is a list of ten words. List at least two words or phrases that are synonymous with the provided word. State whether each synonym you list has a strongly negative, strongly positive, mildly negative, mildly positive, or neutral connotation. Then, use each word in a sentence that indicates the emotional connotation of the word.

1. LEGACY

    Synonym: **Emotional connotation:**

    Sentence:

    Synonym: **Emotional connotation:**

    Sentence:

    Synonym: **Emotional connotation:**

    Sentence:

    Synonym: **Emotional connotation:**

    Sentence:

2. **DEBATE**

    Synonym: **Emotional connotation:**

    Sentence:

    Synonym: **Emotional connotation:**

    Sentence:

    Synonym: **Emotional connotation:**

    Sentence:

    Synonym: **Emotional connotation:**

    Sentence:

3. **CELEBRITY**

    Synonym: **Emotional connotation:**

    Sentence:

    Synonym: **Emotional connotation:**

    Sentence:

    Synonym: **Emotional connotation:**

    Sentence:

    Synonym: **Emotional connotation:**

    Sentence:

4. VISION

Synonym: Emotional connotation:

Sentence:

Synonym: Emotional connotation:

Sentence:

Synonym: Emotional connotation:

Sentence:

Synonym: Emotional connotation:

Sentence:

5. MOBILIZE

Synonym: Emotional connotation:

Sentence:

Synonym: Emotional connotation:

Sentence:

Synonym: Emotional connotation:

Sentence:

Synonym: Emotional connotation:

Sentence:

6. FRIGHTENED

Synonym: Emotional connotation:
Sentence:

Synonym: Emotional connotation:
Sentence:

Synonym: Emotional connotation:
Sentence:

Synonym: Emotional connotation:
Sentence:

7. PRESERVE

Synonym: Emotional connotation:
Sentence:

Synonym: Emotional connotation:
Sentence:

Synonym: Emotional connotation:
Sentence:

Synonym: Emotional connotation:
Sentence:

8. FLAW

Synonym: Emotional connotation:

Sentence:

Synonym: Emotional connotation:

Sentence:

Synonym: Emotional connotation:

Sentence:

Synonym: Emotional connotation:

Sentence:

9. LIMIT (VERB)

Synonym: Emotional connotation:

Sentence:

Synonym: Emotional connotation:

Sentence:

Synonym: Emotional connotation:

Sentence:

Synonym: Emotional connotation:

Sentence:

10. SHALLOW

Synonym: Emotional connotation:

Sentence:

Synonym: Emotional connotation:

Sentence:

Synonym: Emotional connotation:

Sentence:

Synonym: Emotional connotation:

Sentence:

Exercise 3: Creating a Variety of Emotional Effects Through Language Use

Imagine you have purchased an expensive, name-brand portable MP3 player that proved to be defective when you got home and tried to use it. When you returned it to the store, you were told to deal directly with the manufacturer. When you contacted the manufacturer's technical support, however, no one was able to help you. You still have a non-functioning MP3 player, and you have decided to write a series of letters, hoping someone might be able to help you.

Following is a series of facts connected with the purchase and your experience. Use them as you need to write the letters indicated. After each letter, explain how you created the required emotional effect.

Facts:

Item: Rogers Good-Hear 6 GB MP3 Player
Cost: $179.95 (plus tax)
Note: You also purchased the two-year manufacturer's warranty at an additional
  cost of $27.96. Contract number: ZX2357980LBQ23D

Purchased at: WynnMart Discount Electronics
Date purchased: Thursday, June 22
Problems: Advertised to hold 18 hours of music; holds only 7.
  When playing, many songs stop midway through and begin again.
  Some downloaded songs appear on playlist but will not play.
Date returned to store: Monday, June 26
Spoke with: Customer Relations Associate Kimmy
She told you: Since you had purchased the manufacturer's extended warranty,
  you should contact the manufacturer directly.

Date of first phone call: Monday, June 26
Time of first phone call: 3:47 p.m. E.D.T.
Length of hold time: 18 minutes
Spoke with: Customer Service Representative Eric
He told you: Call technical support
Special detail: Eric tried to transfer you to tech support, but you were
  disconnected.

Date of second phone call: Monday, June 26
Time of second phone call: 4:12 p.m. E.D.T.
Length of hold time: 23 minutes
Spoke with: No one
She/He told you:
Special detail: While being transferred from hold to a tech support person, you were disconnected.

Date of third phone call: Monday, June 26
Time of third phone call: 4:36 p.m. E.D.T.
Length of hold time: 20 minutes
Spoke with: Technical Support Specialist Ryan
He told you: Ryan talked you through deleting every song on your playlist and reinstalling them from your computer.
Special detail: The above process took over an hour. Ryan told you this should take care of the problem, but when you tried to listen to your music, you still had the same problems.

Date of fourth phone call: Tuesday, June 27
Time of fourth phone call: 8:35 a.m. E.D.T.
Length of hold time: 37 minutes
Spoke with: Technical Support Specialist Shirav
He told you: Since you did not purchase the extended warranty, you should return the item to the store where you bought it.

Current status of complaint: You are no nearer a solution to your problem than you were before you attempted to return the item to the store.

1. **Letter 1: Letter of Complaint to Manufacturer**
   This is written Tuesday, June 27, immediately upon ending your conversation with Technical Support Specialist Shirav. You are frustrated and angry, but you also want action taken, so you remain respectful.

   Text of Letter:

   Intended Emotional Effect:

   How did you achieve this effect?

2. **Letter 2: Letter to WynnMart Discount Electronics Corporate Headquarters**
   You wish to inform them of the problem you are having with a product purchased in their store. This letter is also written Tuesday, June 27, after Letter 1.

   Text of Letter:

   Intended Emotional Effect:

   How did you achieve this effect?

3. **Letter 3: An E-mail to Your Best Friend**
   You have calmed down considerably and do not want to vent your anger and frustration at your friend. This is a mildly humorous, possibly sarcastic letter explaining the situation. It is written the evening of Tuesday, June 27.

   Text of Letter:

   Intended Emotional Effect:

   How did you achieve this effect?

4. **Letter 4: A Review of the Product for an Online Retail Database**
Written Saturday, July 1.

Text of Letter:

Intended Emotional Effect:

How did you achieve this effect?

5. **Letter 5: A Review of Rogers' Customer Service and Technical Support for an Online Retail Database**
Written Saturday, July 1.

Text of Letter:

Intended Emotional Effect:

How did you achieve this effect?

6. **Letter 6: A Review of WynnMart Discount Electronics' Customer Service for an Online Retail Database**
Written Saturday, July 1.

Text of Letter:

Intended Emotional Effect:

How did you achieve this effect?

Exercise 4: Identifying and Correcting Errors

Each of the following passages contains errors in grammar, mechanics, and spelling; voice and style; application of rhetorical devices; logic; and emotional effect. Rewrite each of the paragraphs, correcting the errors. Explain why you made the changes you made. You do not need to explain corrections of blatant spelling or grammatical errors.

1. Passage One

Massachusetts Institute of Technology graduate student Amal Dorai and other members of the Pi Tau Zeta "living group" hosted the first-ever (and possibly only) Time Traveler Convention on Saturday, May 7, 2005 on the MIT Campus in Cambridge, Masachussets. Dorai publicized the convention broadly (including a front-page New York Times article and an appearance on TV and encouraged people to help. That was before the actual event took place. "Write the details down on a piece of acid-free paper, and slip them into obscure books in academic libraries!" harped Dorai. "Crave them into a clay tablet! If you write for a newspaper, insert a few details about the convention! Tell your friends, so that word of the convention will be preserved in our oral history!"

Nothing that Time Travel might not be imposible until way long after the Campus of MIT no longer exist, Dorai demands that anyone wanting to help alert the Future of the convention include latitude and longitude information. 42.360007 degrees north latitude, 71.087870 degrees west longitude.

While approximately 400 persons from 2005 attended the event. that included a rock band and lectures by several MIT professors. No "verified time travelers" showed up. (Dorai asked all visitors from the future to bring with them something that would offer "clear proof" of their claim. Among his suggestions were the cure for AIDS and the solution to world poverty.)

The fact that no time travelers appeared at the convention does not bum Dorai out. As word of the convention survives, at any point a tiny bit of a newspaper article or book, or a sound bite from a radio or television interview might catch the attention of a Time Traveler who will then decide to pay us a visit.

Revision:

Explanation(s):

2. Passage Two

An Urban Legend is a story, just like the legends of back in the day, that exists in the Oral Tradition of the nation. They are passed mouthally from person to person, and lots of people stupidly believe tham. And even try to tell you, "This actually happened to someone who's best friends with someone I know." The Movies try to make them all seem like scarie stories about mad lunatics with hooks for hands and teenagers makeing out in parked cars, but really there's all types of stories.

Like the one about the lady who was sitting in her parked car, windows closed, with both her hands on the back of her head, leaning forward, forehead resting on the steering wheel of her car. she looked like she was crying and people were a little afraid to stop and talk to her until one brave soul tapped on her window and asked her "are you alright?" and she said she'd been shot in the head and was sitting there for over an hour holding her brains in.

(They were leaking out the bullet hole in the back of her head.)

She asked the good samurai to call the cops and get her to the hospital before she died. He laughed and laughed and said she was crazy that she hadn't been shot but that a tube of biscuit doe (the kind you slap on the side of the table and the do popps out and you seperate the biscuits and bake them) had bursted open and it was the biscit dogh that she thought was her brain oozing out of her head!!!!!!

(And the popp she herd that she thought was a gunshot was realy the buscit can busting open in the heat of the car it was a summer afternoon and shed left her windows all closed).

As with all urban Legends, this one makes since in a sort of stupid sort of way. We donot find it hard to beleive that the hott air in a car could make the doe in a buscut can expand and ecsplode. The day and age we live in right now today in the twenty first century especially in the cities is frightening and many people are just stressed out and think theyre under attack. (That's why the women was so ready to believe that she was shot.)

Urban legends, than, prove that the Oral Tradition is not dead but still alive and strong and our culture is still rife with stories that we believe or want to believe or fear might be true. In the future, these storys might be writ down and put in books for schoolkids to read just like today we read the stories of Paul Bunyan and his blue ox babe and think how silly and unsophisticated those people were back then.

Well we will seem unsophisticated to them.

Revision:

Explanation(s):

Writing Opportunity: *The Homework Essay: An Exploratory Essay*

So far, all of your writing has been thesis-driven, its purpose to communicate what you knew or believed or to demonstrate that you had independently gained some new knowledge. The exploratory essay is very different in that it is driven by the question instead of a presumed answer to the question. In other words, as the name suggests, you will use the exploratory essay to explore a subject from multiple angles. At the end, you may or may not arrive at a conclusion. It is enough to share with your reader your research and thought process.

Exploratory essays are usually dialectical in nature: They require you to examine antithetical positions, sometimes (but not always) arriving at a synthesis.

Important Points:

- Exploratory essays focus on a question, rather than on a thesis.

- Exploratory essays narrate the steps of your research process and the dialectical thinking that resulted from those steps.

- Exploratory essays address both content questions and rhetorical questions about possible responses to the problem under consideration.

- Exploratory essays usually address the strengths and weaknesses of the various views discussed.

Step 1: *Choose your topic*

Usually, problems make good exploratory topics, especially problems that have persisted year after year, despite our best efforts to solve them. The purpose of the exploratory essay, then, is not to offer a solution to this persistent problem, but to examine the problem's nature, the reason(s) past attempts at solution have not worked.

Conversely, you might want to think about a problem that is very new, one that has not been examined thoroughly, and certainly has not been solved. Again, it will not be the purpose of your essay to advance a solution, but to examine the problem's newness, its complexity, and its implications.

Since the purpose of the exploratory essay is to examine the full complexity of an issue or problem, you do not want to choose a problem that is easily solved or about which you already have a strong opinion. Now is a good time to think about issues or problems about which you are completely ambivalent or about which you know absolutely nothing. This way, your research and thinking will be truly exploratory.

> **Hint:** Even though you will ultimately write about only one problem or issue, it is in your best interest to brainstorm and develop as many possibilities as you can. You do not want to invest too much time on only idea just to discover that you simply don't have much to say about it. It is to your advantage to be able to choose from among several possibilities.

> **Hint:** Even after you've chosen the problem or issue you are going to write about, *do not* discard the others. You still might find that the first one you chose isn't working out, and you'll want to choose another from your list.

> **Time Clue:** Give yourself several days to be able to think freely and creatively and to generate truly workable ideas.

Step 2: *Draft the question your essay is going to explore*

> **Example:**
>
> Should citizens in a free democratic society be *required* to vote?

Step 3: *Brainstorm both the pros and cons of your question*

If you can see only one side to your topic, you need to choose something else, as your exploratory essay will not be successful if you merely argue in favor of requiring citizens to vote. This step, then, guarantees that you will be able to discuss all sides of the issue. Remember, the exploratory essay is not a persuasive essay.

Step 4: *Perform your research and take notes*

Unlike a longer research project, it might be sufficient for you to read a few newspaper and magazine articles as well as consult a few reliable and authoritative web sites. Keep in mind that you want to examine the complexity of the issue or problem, not merely advocate a particular view or solution. Your research, therefore, needs to be balanced.

You also want to make sure you take all three types of notes (directly from sources, responses to sources, original ideas), as your exploratory essay will need to explain your own thought processes as well as present your researched information.

Time Clue: This is the bulk of your essay. For a two-week assignment period, give yourself a full week.

Step 5: *Draft your outline*

The exploratory essay will probably be a chronological narrative of your research and thought process. But consider: Do you want to begin with the question? Do you want to begin with an illustrative anecdote?

Do you want to discuss your narrative in intimate detail or in broad concepts?

Time Clue: Allow yourself one day to draft several versions of an outline.

Step 6: *Write your first draft(s)*

Because the exploratory essay allows for a variety of different approaches, write as many first drafts as you have outlines. This is not too time-consuming a step if you have been careful to gather sufficient information and have already thought carefully about how to present that information.

Time Clue: Writing the first draft—even two or three versions—should not take more than one day.

Step 7: *Revise and rewrite*

Set your drafts aside for the night. You can use that time to ask one or two other people to read them and critique them. When you look at them again, consider the following:

- Is your basic issue or problem of interest to anyone else?
- Do you discuss the issue or problem from multiple sides?
- Do you have a variety of reliable sources for each side?
- Have you succeeded in not rushing to an answer or solution to the problem?
- Have you revealed any of yourself in the essay, describing the evolution of your own thought processes, your own doubts, skepticism, etc.?

Time Clue: Revision and rewriting should not take more than a day.

Step 8: *Your exploratory essay is done. Submit it.*

Applying
the
Third Truth

Powerful writing is painless to read.

3 Simple Truths *and*

6 Essential Traits *of*

Powerful Writing

Enrich see RICH
Facile see EASY
Facsimile see COPY 2.
Factor see COMPONENT
Fad see CRAZE
Fade see DIM
Fan see ENTHUSIAST
Faint see WEAK
Fair 1. Fair, unbiased, just, impartial, equitable: free from suspicion or favoritism for any particular side of an issue

FAIR is characterized by frankness, honesty, and an absence of prejudice—said of persons, character, or conduct; as, a fair man; fair dealing; a fair statement. "I would call it *fair* play." —William Shakespeare. *ant.* unfair, dishonest, prejudiced

UNBIASED is characterized by the absolute absence of prejudice in considering a situation. "The lawyers search for *unbiased* jurors." *ant.* biased, partial, partisan

JUST indicates a sense of righteousness, decency, and virtue when acting and making decisions. "The parties awaited a *just* resolution from the arbitrator." *ant.* unjust, unfair, undeserved

IMPARTIAL indicates complete fairness and an absence of favoritism for any party in making a decision. "Our justice system ensures that the judge will be *impartial* when deciding the sentence." *ant.* partial, prejudiced, one-sided

EQUITABLE stresses fairness and equal treatment. "Our Constitution emphasizes equitable treatment of all citizens under the law." *ant.* inequitable, unfair, unjust, mistreated

Trait Five
Word Choice

Make Yours Better!

The Dow Jones Industrial Average was originally a list of twelve of the major industrial stocks in the United States. Measuring the health of these stocks was supposed to be a way to measure the health of the United States economy. Today, the Dow Jones Industrial Average has thirty stocks from a variety of companies. Although some economists believe it is an outdated way to measure the economy, it is still used as a standard for the stock market.

The Dow Jones was devised by Charles Dow (1851-1902), a journalist, and Edward Jones (1856-1920), a statistician. Originally, it was composed of the stocks of twelve of the main industries in the United States, including cotton, sugar, tobacco, and gas. The number of stocks in the Average did not reach thirty until 1928. The companies included in the Average no longer have to be industrial; the current Index includes Microsoft, Coca-Cola, IBM, and Walt Disney.

When the Average was first published, it stood at 40.94 points. A "point" is essentially one dollar of the average value of the thirty stocks on Dow's list. If the average increases by a certain number of points, that essentially means that the *average value* of the thirty stocks increased by that number of dollars. "The Dow" did not average a thousand points until the 1970s. Today, it averages eleven thousand or more. Its movement up and down has mirrored the political situation of the United States; for instance, after the events of September 11, 2001, the Dow fell almost 1400 points. Sometimes the stocks in the Dow undergo a dramatic change that is not political in cause. On October 19, 1987, the Index fell 22 percent for reasons economists still do not understand. In fact, markets all over the world fell that day. This date is now known as Black Monday.

Because the Dow Jones is calculated by adding the prices of all of the stocks together and dividing by the number of stocks, the average is price-weighted. This means that the higher-priced stocks have more influence on the average. For this reason, some people say that Dow Jones Industrial Average is not an accurate indicator of the true market value of the stocks. In addition, some of the stocks in the Average open later than others, so

▓ The first paragraph clearly explains what the essay is going to be about. The language is simple, but not below the level of the subject matter. Flesch Reading Ease is 56.9.

▓ Notice that the author varies the terms he or she uses to describe the main subject. Flesch Reading Ease 28.2.

▓ The careful use of the word "essentially" here makes it clear that this explanation is something of an oversimplification —but not a gross distortion—of the process.

■ The writer explains acronyms that may be unfamiliar to the reader. Again, the language is simple, but not simplistic.

the prices calculated in the Average may reflect the end of trading from the day before. Two other averages, the S and P (Standard and Poor) and the NASDAQ (National Association of Securities Dealers Automated Quotations) are said by critics of the Dow to be more accurate averages of the US economy.

Essay Critique

The author of this passage is dealing with a specialized topic for which specific language is appropriate. Therefore, he or she has to be careful to explain terminology to the reader and keep the language varied and accessible, rather than slipping into jargon or repeating the same terms over and over. The author does a good job explaining the subject clearly without using language that is too elementary or too difficult. The overall Flesch Reading Ease score for this essay is 50.9.

This essay receives a score of ⑩ on the:

Word Choice Rubric

14 = ACCOMPLISHED
Word choice, including use of figurative devices, reflects a thorough understanding of the topic and how best to communicate it in order to meet the needs of the audience and the purpose of the writing.

13 = Words are vivid and concrete without sounding forced or overworked. Figurative devices are appropriate and unaffected, adding clarity, meaning, and interest to the essay.

12 = Word choice is specific, clear, and vital. Powerful nouns and verbs replace weaker words and phrases. Similes, metaphors, and allusions are appropriate and add clarity, meaning and interest to the essay. Word choice and use of figurative language is fluent and effective.

11 = Word choice is specific, clear, and appropriate to the audience, topic, and purpose. Specific words replace vague, general terms. Similes, metaphors, allusions, etc.—while at times strained or not fully appropriate—add meaning and interest to the essay.

⑩ = PROFICIENT
Word choice shows evidence of awareness of the needs of the audience and the demands of the topic and purpose. Figurative devices are, for the most part, original and appropriate.

135

Appreciating Absolutes

Answer the following questions. The answers require you to think logically. They do not require any special knowledge of language.

Once something is full, can it be made "more full" ?

Can something be described as "very full"?

Why or why not?

How about empty: once something is empty, can it be made "more empty?"

Can something be described as "very empty"?

Why or why not?

Look up the word *unique* in the dictionary, and write the definition:

If something is unique, can it be made *more* unique or *less* unique?

Can something be described as "very unique"?

Why or why not?

The point is that, while most adjectives have a positive, comparative, and superlative degree, some adjectives do not. They are called *absolutes* because their meaning is absolute, complete, and definite without any need for emphasis.

Consider the following adjectives:

absolute	favorite	pregnant
boiling	flat	prime
boundless	freezing	rectangular
chief	full	round
complete	impossible	square
closed	limitless	starving
complete	main	straight
dead	parallel	true
double	perfect	unique
entire	penniless	whole
false		

In each of the above cases (and quite a few more), it is impossible to insert the word "more" or "less" before the adjective in any meaningful way. Once someone is penniless, there can not be anyone *more penniless*. And anyone claiming to be *less penniless* simply isn't penniless!

One object cannot be *more perfect* than another. The objects are either perfect or not.

Two amounts are either *equal* or not. Consider George Orwell's famous line: "All animals are equal, but some animals are more equal than others" (*Animal Farm*, 1945). This statement maintains its irony only if the word *equal* remains an absolute.

Since absolute adjectives are non-gradable—that is, they do not have comparative or superlative degrees—a writer's desire to qualify them [As an example: The line Chantal drew is *straighter* than mine.] usually indicates that he or she has chosen the wrong adjective.

Exercise 1: Using Absolutes Correctly

Revise each of the following sentences to eliminate the incorrectly modified absolute with a word or phrase that accurately reflects what the writer wants to express. Then, explain why you changed the adjective as you did. (NOTE: For most of the following sentences, there will be more than one possible revision. It is important, however, that you understand the reason for the revision you choose to make.)

For example:

Althea's bucket was *fuller* than Desmond's.

Revision: *Althea's bucket had more apples in it than Desmond's.*

Explanation: *One bucket cannot be "more full" than another—full is full—but someone might assume that the one basket was "fuller" because it had a higher number of items in it.*

---

1. I've never received a *more perfect* report card.

Revision:

Explanation:

---

2. The invention of a flying machine might have seemed impossible, but the invention of a time machine seems even *more impossible.*

Revision:

Explanation:

3. Chocolate is my *most favorite* flavor of ice cream.

Revision:

Explanation:

4. Circles are *rounder* than ovals.

Revision:

Explanation:

5. While all of the witnesses told untruths, the testimony of the prosecution's chief witness was the *most false* of them all.

Revision:

Explanation:

6. Which is *more true:* cigarette smoking leads to cancer or that eating fatty foods causes heart disease?

Revision:

Explanation:

7. You won't find a *more complete* beginner's package anywhere!

Revision:

Explanation:

9. The burglar was able to enter the house through the *least closed* window.

Revision:

Explanation:

10. Surprisingly, Toni read the newspaper *more completely* than her father.

Revision:

Explanation:

Exception:

Sometimes, the desire to modify an absolute comes from the fact that the item being described does not *fully* contain the quality of the adjective, but *almost* does. By the same token, when comparing two or more items, the writer might want to indicate that one of the items contains the quality of the adjective *more so* than the other(s).

Here is where you need to make a choice as a writer. Common usage might allow you to grade the non-gradable adjective: Anita's haircut was *more perfect* than Brie's.

But, your most formal and academic settings, your most public settings, the settings in which you want to establish that—as an accomplished writer—you know how to be absolutely precise in your word choice will demand that you show more care and understanding of what the words you are using really mean.

Therefore, although one object cannot be *more perfect* than another, the one might be *more* nearly *perfect.* The assumption is that perfection—the absolute—has not been attained, but is approached, and the one object comes closer to the standard.

Exercise 2: Correcting Absolutes

Revise each of the sentences below to eliminate the incorrectly modified absolute with a word or phrase that more accurately reflects what the writer wants to express. Then, explain why you changed the adjective as you did. (NOTE: In some cases, the "more nearly" solution will work. In others, you will still have to make the judgment about what the writer of the original sentence meant and revise the sentence to reflect that more accurately.)

1. I've never received a *more perfect* report card: four A's and one A-minus.

   Revision:

   Explanation:

2. Hector gave Monique a *fuller* glass of soda than he gave Misha.

   Revision:

   Explanation:

3. While at the convention, countless philosophers argued about whose theory was more *absolute*.

   Revision:

   Explanation:

4. The circles Jamie drew with the protractor are *rounder* than the ones Clovis drew freehand.

Revision:

Explanation:

5. Some parents treat their younger and older children *more equally* than other parents do.

Revision:

Explanation:

6. Latitude lines are called "parallels" because they are *more parallel* than longitude lines.

Revision:

Explanation:

7. This is the *most complete* set of instructions I have ever seen!

Revision:

Explanation:

8. Sean used the protractor to be sure his angles are *more square* in this diagram than in his last.

Revision:

Explanation:

9. The *rounder* the moon gets, the closer to full it is.

Revision:

Explanation:

10. Janet said it was *more freezing* inside the cabin than it was outside.

Revision:

Explanation:

There are times when you've heard or seen absolutes modified by "very" to add emphasis: "That's very true." This use is unnecessary. Once something it true, or full, or complete, or wrong, the absolute meaning of the word does not need emphasis. A *very true* statement is *no truer* than a true statement.

Consider "flaming" in a chat room, on a list serve, or while instant messaging. The use of CAPITAL LETTERS in those contexts indicates a raised voice—shouting. To flame ONCE IN A WHILE might be helpful in making yourself heard or emphasizing your point. WHEN YOU OVERUSE THE CAPITAL LETTERS, HOWEVER, YOU COMPLETELY DESTROY THE EMPHASIS AND ACTUALLY MAKE YOUR WORDS DIFFICULT AND UNPLEASANT TO READ. Rather than drawing attention to you message, you might actually find yourself ignored.

As an accomplished writer, you need to know when it's all right for something to be very true, perfectly true, or absolutely true and when to let it be just plain old *true*.

Imaged-Based vs. Concept-Based Words

In 2001, Cynthia G. Emrich, an assistant professor at Perdue University, along with Holly H. Brower of Butler University, Jack M. Feldman of the Georgia Institute of Technology, and Howard Garland of the University of Delaware, conducted research on why certain United States Presidents were generally regarded as charismatic while others were not. Why did some presidents seem to have an indefinable charm that made the general public like them, despite known character flaws or problems in their administrations?

What the researchers found was that, in their speeches, charismatic presidents used a significantly higher proportion of "image-based" words than "concept-based" words.

Image-based words found in the speeches of charismatic presidents include:

heart
hand
journey
dream

Concept-based words include:

commitment
help
endeavor
idea

Using Visual Terms

In their 2001 report, Emerich and her team quote a speech delivered by President John F. Kennedy, regarded as one of the most charismatic presidents of the twentieth century: "Together let us explore *the stars*, conquer *the desert*, eradicate *disease*, tap the *ocean depths*, and encourage the arts and commerce" [Italics added to illustrate the use of "image-based" words].

By contrast, Jimmy Carter, one of the twentieth century's least charismatic presidents, delivered the following line: "Let our recent *mistakes* bring a *resurgent commitment* to the *basic principles* of our nation, for we know that if we *despise* our government, we have no *future*" [Italics added to illustrate the use of concept-based words].

Clearly, then, as we began to establish as early as Book One, using language that is seen as clear and concrete will result in both you and your work's being received more favorably.

Compare President Jimmy Carter's original sentence with a suggested revision:

Original:

Let our recent *mistakes* bring a *resurgent commitment* to the *basic principles* of our nation, for we know that if we *despise* our government, we have no *future*.

Revision:

Let the crimes of the previous administration motivate us to renew our commitment to rule by law and equal justice for all; for we know that if the common citizen cannot trust his or her government, the nation is doomed.

Exercise 3: Revising with Images

Revise the following sentences to replace all of the concept-based words with image-based words.

For example:

Original: To consider both sides of the issue is not a sign of weakness.

Revision: *To sit down and listen to both sides of an issue is a sign of strength.*

1. We must all work hard and keep the goal in sight.

2. An employer has a right to ask his or her employees to be dependable and to help the company meet its goals.

3. While we do not need to agree with it, we must all endeavor to understand the other person's point of view.

4. There is no alternative but to renew our commitment to our established priorities.

5. Tracing the rumor to its source will help alleviate its damage.

6. Just think of the possibilities.

7. Great effort will produce great results.

8. If you are agreeable to my suggestion, we will proceed.

9. The president's idea is to free society of its ills.

10. It is important to enquire into the central issue before voicing an opinion.

Balancing the Rational and the Emotional

Communication has two main components: the rational and the emotional. The formal, academic writing you've done in school and the type of writing you'll do in college or work will mostly communicate rationally—about hard data and facts. Pages and pages of recited facts, however, can be tortuous for your reader to get through and for your teacher to grade. Your job as writer is to make certain you not only present the information accurately and with authority, but also present the information so it can be understood and remembered.

One essential way to keep your reader engaged is to pause in your recitation of information to provide an interpretation of that information. If you leave it to your readers to make sense of the information on their own—especially highly technical information—you are allowing them to arrive at their own conclusions. Readers will always filter the information through their own experiences and beliefs, but, by providing *your* interpretation of the facts, you guide them to consider *your* conclusions.

Consider the research paper. You have read countless pages of facts, dates, statistics, case studies; you have "surfed the web" dry; you've interviewed experts in the field and watched every video and DVD available on your subject. In short, you have become something of an expert. Now, you need to share that information with someone else, to explain to your teacher what you have learned during the course of your research. Clearly, you will want to share the facts. After all, facts are what give your thesis its credibility. But to show that you actually learned something, you need also to explain the significance of the facts. Think of your reader like a student you are teaching. He or she wants someone knowledgeable to point out the implications of the rational data.

Exercise 4: Interpreting Data

Following are several lists of facts and data gathered during a research project. Offer some interpretation of the data. Explain what you would want your reader to conclude if you were presenting this information in a paper.

When choosing the words to state your interpretation, you will want to be especially careful to avoid unwanted emotional connotations.

For example:

The earth completes one 360° rotation on its axis in twenty-four hours. The period of one complete axial rotation is called a *day*. The earth completes 365 ¼ rotations for every one full orbit around the sun. A period of 365 days is called a *year*.

Interpretation(s):

A year is actually 365 1/4 days long. At the beginning of a new year, the earth is not in the same place it was relative to the sun on the beginning of the previous year.

Scientists can measure very accurately when the sun will be in a certain position relative to the earth. The two times each year when the sun is directly over the equator are called equinoxes. The time each year when the sun is directly over the Tropic of Cancer is called the summer solstice. The time each year when the sun is directly over the Tropic of Capricorn is called the winter solstice.

Interpretation(s):

At the beginning of a new year, the earth is not in the same place it was relative to the sun on the beginning of the previous year. The dates of the equinoxes and solstices will move forward every year due to the discrepancy between the earth's 365 1/4-day orbit and the 365-day calendar.

To keep track of the passing of time and to be able to discuss events in the past, present, and the future, we mark the beginning of a new year every 365 days. We use the equinoxes and solstices to mark the beginnings of the four seasons. Certain days and events are fixed in the calendar (Christmas on December 25, Thanksgiving in November, etc.) and associated with certain seasons (Thanksgiving is an autumn/harvest festival, May Day is a spring festival).

Interpretation(s):

Not only will the dates of the equinoxes and solstices move forward every year, but, eventually seasons will occur during odd months (May would be winter, October spring, etc.) Seasonal holidays will fall either out of season or in odd months (Thanksgiving in February, May Day in August, etc.)

List 1:

- Energy from the sun heats the earth's surface, and the earth radiates some of this energy back into space.

    Interpretation(s):

- Greenhouse gases in the atmosphere (water vapor, carbon dioxide, and other gases) trap some of the outgoing energy, retaining heat like the glass panels of a greenhouse.

    Interpretation(s):

- Natural processes like plant respiration and the decomposition of organic matter release more than 10 times the CO2 (carbon dioxide) released by human activities.

    Interpretation(s):

- Without this natural "greenhouse effect," temperatures would be much lower than they are:

- Life as we know it would not be possible.

- Because of naturally-occurring greenhouse gases, the earth's average temperature is 60°F.

   Interpretation(s):

- Since the beginning of the Industrial Revolution, the concentration of carbon dioxide in the atmosphere has increased nearly 30%.

- The concentration of methane gas has more than doubled.

- Nitrous oxide concentrations have risen by about 15%.

   Interpretation(s):

- As a result of the Industrial Revolution, the burning of coal, oil, and natural gas (called "fossil fuels") has significantly increased the amount of carbon dioxide released into the atmosphere.

   Interpretation(s):

- Fossil fuels burned to run cars and trucks, heat homes and businesses, and power factories are responsible for about:

   o 98% of U.S. carbon dioxide emissions

   o 24% of methane emissions

   o 18% of nitrous oxide emissions.

   Interpretation(s):

- Environmental scientists project that, by the year 2100, carbon dioxide concentrations will be 30-150% higher than today's levels.

  Interpretation(s):

- The 20th century's 10 warmest years all occurred in the last 15 years of the century.
- 1998 was the warmest year on record.

  Interpretation(s):

- The snow cover in the Northern Hemisphere and floating ice in the Arctic Ocean have decreased.

  Interpretation(s):

- Globally, the sea level has risen 4-8 inches over the past century.

  Interpretation(s):

- Worldwide, precipitation over land has increased by about one percent.

  Interpretation(s):

- The average global temperature has increased by almost 1°F over the past century.

  Interpretation(s):

- Scientists expect the average global temperature to increase an additional 2 to 6°F over the next one hundred years.

   Interpretation(s):

- At the peak of the last ice age, the temperature was only 7°F colder than it is today, and glaciers covered much of North America.

   Interpretation(s):

Source: *United States Environmental Protection Agency Global Warming Site*

2. List 2:

- 103,812,000 **males** over 18 years of age according to 2000 census: 64% of this population registered to vote in 2004 national election

   6,411,000 with less than ninth-grade education
   31.7% of this population registered to vote in 2004 national election
   73.6% of registered voters in this population actually voted in 2004 national election

   10, 297,000 attended grades 9 – 12 without a high school diploma
   41.0% of this population registered to vote in 2004 national election
   76% of registered voters in this population actually voted in 2004 national election

   32,817,000 received high school diploma
   58.9% of this population registered to vote in 2004 national election
   84% of registered voters in this population actually voted in 2004 national election

   26,562,000 attended some college or attained an associate's degree
   72.1% of this population registered to vote in 2004 national election
   88.7% of registered voters in this population actually voted in 2004 national election

17,819,000 completed a bachelor's degree
77.4 % of this population registered to vote in 2004 national election
93.7% of registered voters in this population actually voted in 2004 national election

9,915,000 completed (an) advanced degree(s)
78.6% of this population registered to vote in 2004 national election
96.4% of registered voters in this population actually voted in 2004 national election

Interpretation(s):

- 111,882,000 **females** over 18 years of age according to 2000 census:
  60.1% of this population registered to vote in 2004 national election

6,164,000 with less than ninth-grade education
33.4% of this population registered to vote in 2004 national election
71.6% of registered voters in this population actually voted in 2004 national election

10,422,000 attended grades 9 – 12 without a high school diploma
49.5% of this population registered to vote in 2004 national election
75% of registered voters in this population actually voted in 2004 national election

35,728,000 received high school diploma
64% of this population registered to vote in 2004 national election
85.9% of registered voters in this population actually voted in 2004 national election

32,350,000 attended some college or attained an associate's degree
75% of this population registered to vote in 2004 national election
90% of registered voters in this population actually voted in 2004 national election

18,780,000 completed a bachelor's degree
76.5 % of this population registered to vote in 2004 national election
95% of registered voters in this population actually voted in 2004 national election

8,437,000 completed (an) advanced degree(s)
82% of this population registered to vote in 2004 national election
96.4% of registered voters in this population actually voted in 2004 national election

Source: *U.S. Census Bureau, Population Division, Education & Social Stratification Branch*

Interpretation(s):

Additional or Overall Interpretation(s):

The other key factor in dealing with images is emotion. Depending on your thesis, facts and data may provide your readers reason to act. Emotion, however, provides the motivation for action. Don't think that it is thoroughly inappropriate to consider the emotional aspect of communication in an academic paper because, as has already been discussed, your reader will automatically filter the information you present through his or her prior knowledge, experience, and emotions. Just as you must share your interpretation of the facts you present, you must also indicate the emotional response or connection you are looking for.

This emotional impact is often best created through symbols. As Dr. Emerich and her co-researchers discovered in their study of the speeches of charismatic presidents, the use of strong but familiar words that create images in people's minds is essential to composing a powerful, moving, and memorable message. Thus, visual symbols are the key to tapping into your readers' emotions as your facts and data tap into their intellects.

Exercise 5: Interpreting the Emotional Impact of Metaphors in Writing

Each of the following groups contains three sentences that say essentially the same thing. For each group, choose which of the three sentences you think is the strongest and explain why.

For example:

The teacher's siren of a voice awoke Charles from his back-of-the-room slumber.

The teacher's warning bell of a voice awoke Charles from his back-of-the-room slumber.

The teacher's alarm of a voice awoke Charles from his back-of-the-room slumber.

Strongest Sentence: *The teacher's siren of a voice awoke Charles from his back-of-the-room slumber.*

Reason(s): *Everyone is familiar with the loud, shrill sound of a police or fire siren. "Warning bell," and "alarm" are too general—are they loud and clanging? Deep and tolling like old-fashioned church bells? Shrill, little bells? "Siren" is a much more specific comparison to the teacher's obviously loud and alarming voice.*

1. I want good grades, but I refuse to be an employee of my books and teachers.

I want good grades, but I refuse to be a servant to my books and teachers.

I want good grades, but I refuse to be a slave to my books and teachers.

Strongest Sentence:

Reason(s):

2. Without a doubt, reading provides the entrance to new worlds.

Without a doubt, reading opens the door to new worlds.

Without a doubt, reading is the key to new worlds.

Strongest Sentence:

Reason(s):

3. It is important for parents to give their children both a sense of security and the freedom to live their own lives.

It is important for parents to give their children both security and freedom.

It is important for parents to give their children both roots and wings.

Strongest Sentence:

Reason(s):

4. *The Dummy's Guide to Software Applications* is an essential book for the computer-using layperson.

The Dummy's Guide to Software Applications has everything the computer-using layperson needs to use his or her computer more effectively.

The Dummy's Guide to Software Applications is the computer-using layperson's Bible.

Strongest Sentence:

Reason(s):

5. Dr. Shilomo's course weeds out the students who are not suited to study her field.

Dr. Shilomo's course is a test to establish which students are suited for her field and which are not.

Dr. Shilomo's course butchers the many students who simply are not suited to study her field.

Strongest Sentence:

Reason(s):

Exercise 6: Interpreting the Emotional Impact of Metaphors in Writing

Following are five pairs of sentences. The two sentences in a pair share the same topic, but each one creates a different emotional impact because of the nature of the metaphor. Explain the suggested emotion, and then discuss the appropriate audience and purpose of each particular emotional connection.

1. Mr. Wordsley's search for cheaters became a crusade.

Emotional Impact:

Appropriate Use:

Mr. Wordsley's search for cheaters became a witch hunt.

Emotional Impact:

Appropriate Use:

2. Reading is the path to enlightenment.

Emotional Impact:

Appropriate Use:

Reading is the highway to enlightenment.

Emotional Impact:

Appropriate Use:

3. Hermione planted a few seeds of thought in her colleagues' minds at the meeting yesterday.

Emotional Impact:

Appropriate Use:

Hermione infected her colleagues' minds with the germ of a idea at the meeting yesterday.

Emotional Impact:

Appropriate Use:

4. After years of patient study, Norcross' talent began to blossom.

Emotional Impact:

Appropriate Use:

After years of patient study, Norcross' talent began to blaze.

Emotional Impact:

Appropriate Use:

5. Have you noticed how Azar showers Amelie with affection?

Emotional Impact:

Appropriate Use:

Have you noticed how Azar drowns Amelie in affection?

Emotional Impact:

Appropriate Use:

Extending the Metaphor

It is even more powerful to extend the metaphor as a recurring concept to help establish subsequent images.

For example, you may have tried to explain the job of a school principal in terms of the captain of a cruise ship. Once you've established that comparison, you can further develop your point with other nautical metaphors. For example, the teachers become stewards, the students passengers, and the curriculum might be compared to the maps and charts used to navigate the ship to the promised destination.

Such extended metaphors can be very helpful both in explaining rational information as well as establishing an emotional appeal. Be careful, however, that you do not push your extended metaphor to ridiculous extremes. For example, "The school's rules and regulations are the planks of wood on the ship's deck; the school district administration and school board are the executives of the cruise line, etc. You must also be careful not to mix your metaphor—at least not in the same paragraph (e.g., "We're all in the same boat here, so let's haul anchor and soar to new heights of academic excellence.")

Be careful not to confuse your reader with mixed metaphors.

I had reached the end of my rope, but saw the light at the end of the tunnel and knew we were all in the same boat after all.

Exercise 7: Creating the Extended Metaphor

In earlier books of this series, you practiced creating authentic metaphors and similes— original comparisons relevant to your own life and experience. Brainstorm and list new ones. Then, list the elements of each term that could be used to extend the metaphor in the development of your explanation. Finally, explain the emotion conveyed in the metaphor.

For example:

Metaphor: *Comparing a book to a movie based on that book? You might as well eat a gourmet meal prepared by a short-order cook!*

Elements: *Novelist = gourmet creator of recipe; screenwriter = cook. Rich imagery, subtle and deep character development, multiple plot levels of novel = rare and expensive ingredients found in specialty stores. Plot and character development of movie = bottled spices and packaged mixes from grocery store. Experience of reading, pausing, reflecting = time in five-star restaurant to enjoy gourmet meal. Ninety-minute movie, noisy theater = gobbling sandwich at fast-food restaurant*

Emotion: *Clearly, the writer feels disdain for movie versions of books.*

1. **Metaphor:**

   Elements:

   Emotion:

2. **Metaphor:**

    Elements:

    Emotion:

3. **Metaphor:**

    Elements:

    Emotion:

4. **Metaphor:**

    Elements:

    Emotion:

5. **Metaphor:**

    Elements:

    Emotion:

More Fun With Idioms, Slang, and Clichés

Quick Review:

An **idiom** is an expression that does not make literal sense, such as "hitting below the belt" and "ballpark figure." An overuse of idioms can make your writing too informal or conversational and can make it difficult for readers who do not understand the idiom to follow your thoughts.

A **cliché** is any expression that has been overused. "I haven't a clue," is a good example. Chances are, you are using the cliché instead of really thinking about the most powerful way to make your point.

Slang is informal, too likely to change, and appeals to too narrow an audience to be appropriate for all but the most personal writing.

Exercise 8: Correcting Clichés

Each of the following phrases is a common cliché. Explain the expression's meaning or origin. Then, offer a fresh, original, and clever replacement.

For example:

Against the grain.

Explanation: In woodworking, to cut material "against the grain" of the wood causes excessive wear to tools and results in rough, jagged edges. It is easier and makes neater cuts to cut with the grain of the wood. Thus, to go "against the grain" is to take a less easy way and possibly to produce less satisfactory results.

Replacement: climb the down escalator

1. Fresh as a daisy

Explanation:

Replacement:

2. Pure as the driven snow

Explanation:

Replacement:

3. Crack of dawn

   Explanation:

   Replacement:

4. Between a rock and a hard place

   Explanation:

   Replacement:

5. Break new ground

   Explanation:

   Replacement:

6. Broad daylight

   Explanation:

   Replacement:

7. Common ground

Explanation:

Replacement:

8. Cover a lot of ground

Explanation:

Replacement:

9. Cut and dried

Explanation:

Replacement:

10. Dead of winter

Explanation:

Replacement:

11. Don't put the cart before the horse

Explanation:

Replacement:

12. Down to earth

Explanation:

Replacement:

13. A drop in the bucket

Explanation:

Replacement:

14. Sink or swim

Explanation:

Replacement:

15. Fertile ground

Explanation:

Replacement:

Avoiding Personal Clichés

By now, you have probably compiled a fairly impressive portfolio of work from freshman year to the present. This portfolio not only records your past accomplishments and growth as a writer, it can also help you diagnose your own weaknesses and plan your continued improvement.

From your portfolio, select two papers each from your freshman through junior years. Then, select one paper from your senior year.

Read each of these papers carefully, and write down any words, phrases, sentences, or expressions that appear in more than two different papers, especially if they appear in papers from more than one year. These are your personal clichés, words you default to even if there are more vivid or precise terms you could use.

Clichés are a sure sign of a lazy, unimaginative writer.

"It was a dark and stormy night, and the weather outside wasn't fit for man or beast, so the lovesick maiden battened down the hatches and beat a hasty retreat into her bedroom."

Exercise 9: Eliminating Personal Clichés

List five of your personal clichés. Then, explain what meaning you intend to convey by the phrase, and write a newer and fresher way to express that meaning.

For example:

Personal Cliché: *drew a deep breath*

Explanation: *to take in air, breathe deeply, inhale, maybe showing exhaustion, sadness, or resignation*

Replacement(s): *inhaled deeply; inhaled greedily; greedily filled [his/her] lungs with air*

Personal Cliché: *would seem to indicate that*

Explanation: *the evidence suggests; maybe only mildly suggests; certainly not strong enough to prove or establish conclusively*

Replacement(s): *indicates; suggests; points to the conclusion that*

1. Personal Cliché:

  Explanation:

  Replacement(s):

2. **Personal Cliché:**

Explanation:

Replacement(s):

3. **Personal Cliché:**

Explanation:

Replacement(s):

4. **Personal Cliché:**

Explanation:

Replacement(s):

5. **Personal Cliché:**

Explanation:

Replacement(s):

Writing Opportunity: *The Research Paper/Extended Essay: The Abstract*

What is an Abstract?

An abstract is a summary of an essay or paper in a single paragraph, roughly 350 words in length. It expresses the main idea or argument of the paper and briefly highlights the major points. Throughout your education and career, you might have occasion to write abstracts of your own work as well as abstracts of others' work. In Book One "Novice", you abstracted an article written by someone else. Now you will write an abstract for your own work.

This kind of abstract can be written at any time during the writing of the paper—often writing a draft of the abstract *first* allows you to focus your research and development on your clearly-stated intent—but an abstract is intended to be read first. The final draft of the abstract, however, should not be completed until after the paper is done.

The abstract explains why you did a particular project. (To say you were merely filling a course requirement is *not* sufficient reason!) The abstract also summarizes your conclusions, explains briefly what those conclusions mean, and how you arrived at them.

The abstract should include those points that you want your reader to remember even after he or she has forgotten most of the details of your discussion. Do not refer in the abstract to information that is not in the actual paper.

The abstract can also be a useful tool for you to check that you have a clear understanding of your thesis and main points. If you can state your thesis and main idea clearly in a few sentences, so that someone who's not familiar with your subject can still understand the main idea, then you have a good grasp of the ideas you are trying to express. An abstract includes everything of central importance and gives the reader a clear overview of what the full paper says.

The abstract also functions as something like a map of the full paper. Just as in several of the other writing opportunities in this and previous books, you used your outline to diagnose problems in your intended paper and shared early drafts of your paper with other readers, you can share your abstract with people you trust, who don't have time to read through an entire draft of your paper. By looking at a well-written abstract, your reader can quickly determine the gist of your paper. Since abstracts are brief, you can reasonably ask a reader to look at several drafts as your thinking and writing evolve.

If you are writing an abstract as part of an essay for a humanities class, you will place it on a separate page, just after the title page just before the essay itself.

Points to consider when planning and writing your abstract:

- An abstract will almost always be read along with the title of the paper, so do not simply repeat or rephrase the title. The abstract will, however, most likely be read before or instead of the complete paper, so make it complete enough to stand on its own.

- Your readers expect you to summarize your conclusions as well as your purpose, methods, and main findings. Give the different points the same emphasis in the abstract that they receive in the actual paper.

- Avoid using first person.

- Choose active constructions rather than passive ones (*a close examination of the text revealed* rather than *it was revealed by a close examination of the text*).

- Avoid trade names, acronyms, abbreviations, or symbols. You would need to explain them, and that would take too much space. Remember that you are limited to a single paragraph, 300 – 350 words.

- It has also become very important in professional and academic circles to use "key words" in an abstract. When your paper and abstract are published electronically, other researchers will perform key word searches for information. If your abstract does not contain many of the key words reflecting the content of your paper, it will not appear on these researchers' lists.

Criteria required in an abstract:

- **purpose of paper being abstracted**
  - o What is the author's reason for writing?
  - o What is the author's main idea?

- **scope of paper being abstracted**
  - o What is the focus in the paper being abstracted?

- **method of research**
  - o What kinds of evidence does the author of the paper provide?
  - o How does the author of the paper try to convince the reader that his or her main idea is valid?

- **results**
  - o What are the consequences of the problem or issue that the author is discussing?

- **recommendations**
  - o What solutions (new interpretations, call to action, etc.) does the author of the paper present?

- **conclusions**
  - o What does the author ultimately conclude about the issue based on his or her research and study?

Remember that—if you are writing an abstract of your own work—*you* are "the author" referred to above.

Step 1: *Choose the paper, essay, or article to abstract*

Since this abstract is going to be drawn from a paper you yourself have written, you might want to consider using one of the essays you wrote in either Trait 3 (the dialectic) or Trait 4 (the exploratory essay). Or your teacher may want to assign you to abstract something else you have written this year.

Step 2: *Outline the key points of the essay you are abstracting*

You will probably find it helpful to actually highlight or underline what you consider to be the main points of your essay as you reread it. If you still have your outline, consult it to see what information is included in the main headings.

Step 3: *Write down your purpose and scope statements*

What is the author's reason for writing?
What is the author's main idea?
What is the focus in the paper being abstracted?

Step 4: *List the key words you need to use*

Think what key words a researcher might type into the search engine to arrive at your essay.

Step 5: *Write your first draft*

Use the format suggested above. Remember that the abstract is more than merely a summary or synopsis of the paper, but actually highlights the *process* of research and discussion as much as it encapsulates the information.

> **Time Clue:** This should take no more than 15 or 20 minutes. You have the original essay and your own notes to help you. There is no need for original thought in this step.

Step 6: *Share your draft with at least one other person*

Does the draft meet the criteria of an abstract? Does this reader feel as if he or she can judge from the abstract whether reading the entire paper will be helpful?

Step 7: *Review your draft*

Does what you've written accurately and adequately reflect your goals and intentions for the essay you are abstracting?

Step 8: *Write your final draft*

Again, this should not be a long or difficult step. If you put the necessary thought and planning into the original essay and had a clear sense of your point and purpose when you wrote the original essay, and if you have carefully reread it, you should not be straining for any new ideas or material now.

Remember that your abstract does *not* provide any of the documentation that appears in your actual paper.

Step 9: *Turn in your paper.*

Trait Six

Voice

TRAIT SIX:
VOICE

> *Go with what seems inevitable in your own heritage.*
> *Embrace it and it may lead you to eloquence.*
> —**William Zinsser, *On Writing Well***

Make Yours Better!

Complex and confusing as contemporary politics can be—trying to keep track of multiple parties, factions within parties, and the ebb and flow of power and influence within a faction, party, or legislative body—twenty-first-century power-mongerers have nothing on the kingmakers of fifteenth-century England. This was a time when a dispute over succession to the throne led to six changes of administration within a thirty-year period. This may be normal for the United States, which changes its "ruler" every four years, but was unheard-of for England whose monarchs ruled until they died. There were several different groups—all within a single family—bickering over who had the stronger claim to the throne. The battles of this time are now called "The Wars of the Roses."

The two main factions, each symbolized by the use of a different color of rose as its insignia, were the Yorks and the Lancastrians. The Yorks (white roses) were the party of Richard Plantagenet, Duke of York. Richard was descended from King Edward III of England and had a strong claim to the throne. On the other side were King Henry VI, his queen, Margaret of Anjou, and the Lancasters (red roses). Henry VI was also descended from Edward III, but his claim to the throne was questionable because his grandfather, King Henry IV, had seized power by overthrowing King Richard II.

At the time the Wars of the Roses started, England was feeling the defeat of the Hundred Years' War with France. This was an expensive and disastrous series of battles over English holdings in France. By the end, England had lost almost all of its land in France. Because of these losses and because of genetic tendencies, in 1453, Henry VI went crazy. "Uncle" Richard briefly took his place, but then Henry recovered. On May 22, 1455, the forces of

---

- An emotion-laden word like "mongerer" and the informal expression "have nothing on" begin to establish a less-academic and somewhat judgmental tone. This author is going to be, at least mildly, critical of the people and events discussed in this essay.

- The author continues the comparison to our own political system, which makes the subject more accessible.

- The emphasis that the warring factions were related, the informal use of dashes to set this phrase apart from the rest of the sentence, and the use of the word "bickering" all maintain the mildly sarcastic voice the author has adopted.

- The author gives us the events of this historical period as if he or she is telling a story. Instead of simple dates and facts, we get a real human voice. Use of the near-slang word "crazy" instead of the more formal "insane" and referring to Richard, Duke of York, as "Uncle" Richard reinforces the lightly mocking tone.

Henry and Richard clashed at the Battle of St. Albans. The Wars were on. Hank was captured by Rich, and Queen Maggie fled into exile in Wales.

Soon however, with the help of Henry's half-brother, Jasper Tudor, Maggie gathered an army and returned. In 1460, her forces defeated those of Richard. In fact, the Duke of York was killed in the battle, and Margaret ordered that his head be placed on a pike overlooking the town of York.

But the death of white-rose Richard was not the end of the red-roses' problems. Richard's son, Edward, who was very intelligent and very popular, now had his father's claim to the throne. There was also another man on the scene: Richard Neville, Earl of Warwick, probably the most powerful man in London after the royal family. Neville seized control of London and had Edward crowned King Edward IV in 1461. Margaret and her forces were defeated by King Edward's forces at the Battle of Towton, on March 4, 1461, and she again fled the country.

But it was still not the end! Edward IV and Richard Neville began fighting over, of all things, which woman the king would marry. Neville rebelled against Edward. One-time enemies Richard Neville and Margaret of Anjou (remember Queen Maggie?) now formed an alliance, even arranging the marriage of her son and his daughter. Unfortunately for them, it was not to be. Neville was killed at the Battle of Barnet on April 14, 1471, while Mags was captured at the Battle of Tewksbury the same year.

Even then, the red-rosed Lancasters were not entirely defeated. The king who ended the Wars of the Roses actually represented the Lancastrian side. He was Henry Tudor, the nephew of that same Jasper Tudor who had helped Margaret in Wales. He defeated Richard III, the brother of Edward IV who had become king when Edward died in 1483. Henry Tudor became King Henry VII and began the Tudor dynasty. He also married Elizabeth of York (Edward IV's daughter), bringing the Yorks and Lancasters together after all this time. And what insignia did he design for his family? Why the Tudor rose, an emblem combining the red and white roses of the formerly feuding families.

Use of nicknames continues the mocking tone. The essay, while historically accurate, is very conversational and narrative.

"White-rose," "red-rose" rather than House names and "man on the scene" continue to maintain the conversational voice.

Even punctuation can be used to maintain voice.

Parenthetical comments and continued use of nicknames reinforce informal, conversational voice.

Essay Critique

The author of this passage creates a strong voice. When you read it, you can sense that the author is interested, even amused, by the subject matter. While such a detailed historical narrative might be confusing and dry, this author uses humor, a touch of sarcasm, and a conversational narrative voice to keep the reader engaged. If there were a flaw here, it might be either that the humorous tone is not fully appropriate for an academic subject, or that the writer is perhaps a little heavy-handed with the humor.

This essay receives a score of 10 on the:

Voice Rubric

14 = ACCOMPLISHED
The narrative voice of the essay is a natural and integral part of the piece, establishing the author's attitude toward the subject and the audience as well as communicating the ideas and information of the essay in a way that invites the reader to continue reading.

13 = **Narrative voice** is a natural result of the writer's language choices and is appropriate for the topic, purpose, and audience.

12 = **The narrative voice** of the essay seems inevitable, given the topic, purpose, and audience. Language is precise and fully controlled.

11 = **The narrative voice** of the essay is consistent and appropriate for the topic, purpose, and audience. Language is precise and fully controlled.

10 = PROFICIENT
Narrative voice is appropriate to the topic, purpose, and audience. Sentences are clear and balanced, but largely overstated or forced—voice for the sake of voice.

A Quick Review of Voice and Tone, and Introducing Style

You already know that voice is the attitude you want to convey toward your reader. Tone is the attitude you want to convey toward your subject. The one voice-tone aspect we have not discussed yet in the *Three Simple Truths* series is *style*. Students often assume that writing style has to do with some indefinite sense of personal style, or personality. Certainly, there are those people who try to explain away poor grammar and mechanics as "style." (Example: I know there are a lot of sentence fragments and run-on sentences in this paper; that's my style.)

Style, however, is a technical term that describes the overall effect a writer creates through every one of his or her individual language choices. Style is an intentional choice; it does not happen by accident or subconsciously. If you are not in complete control of your language use, then you cannot call whatever results your "style."

Your writing should reflect appropriate and consistent choices. The style supports the content—formal (with long sentences, balanced constructions, challenging vocabulary) or informal (conversational or colloquial). The purpose of your writing and your style have an undeniable cause-and-effect relationship.

Your goal in college writing is to understand the material of your discipline and be able to discuss it effectively in writing. Your teacher will want facts as well as your interpretation of those facts. He or she will want to be able to assess, through your writing, how comfortable you are talking about the material you covered in the course. Your goal in most academic writing is to convey facts about a subject, integrate opinions based on facts, and ultimately arrive at a new insight or understanding you can share with your reader.

The impression you make on your reader, such as confidence, authority, fluency, and seriousness, are functions of your style.

Exercise 1: Examining a Variety of Styles

Following are ten expressions of the same meaning. Describe the style of each sentence, and explain how this style is achieved.

For example:

It would almost seem as if the author of the passage were trying to incite both internal and external disharmony.

Style: *formal, academic, evasive*

How Achieved: *"It would almost seem" weakens the point. Use of subjunctive ("as if...were") suggests that this may not be the author's intent. The writer of this statement distances him or herself from the issue.*

One gets the impression that the author's intent is to instigate disagreement between those who hold varying views as well as dissention within the ranks of those who support the legislation.

Style: *formal, academic, direct*

How Achieved: *"One gets" is more direct than "It would almost seem," but still suggests that the point is reader inference more than writer's implication. There is no evasive use of subjunctive. Also, the disagreeing parties are more clearly identified.*

Apparently, the author hopes to create controversy: both between the opposing camps and within the body of supporters.

Style: *less formal (but not overly conversational), direct*

How Achieved: *"Apparently" shifts focus from reader inference to writer implication. "Controversy" is a stronger noun than "disharmony," "disagreement," and "dissention." Use of colon (:) allows for shorter sentence structure.*

I get the impression that Brandon wants to cause trouble between the supporters and non-supporters and even get the non-supporters angry at each other.

Style: *informal, less direct*

How Achieved: *Use of first person shows that the issue is the reader's inference and renders the entire statement informal. "Trouble" is less clear than the more formal "controversy," and "angry" is too vague to communicate exactly what the author (Brandon) wanted to occur in the camp of the supporters.*

Brandon simply wants to tick everyone off.

Style: *slang, informal, emotional, conversational*

How Achieved: *To "tick" someone "off" is a slang expression that many readers might never have encountered. The statement is emotionally strong, clearly states the emotion through writer implication, but does not suggest what the anger is about or between whom.*

1. He's not a particularly good writer.

Style:

How achieved:

2. His skill as a writer leaves much to be desired.

Style:

How achieved:

3. Certainly his mother can take pride in his ability as a writer.

Style:

How achieved:

4. He's a lousy writer.

Style:

How achieved:

5. Many have questioned his capacity as a writer.

Style:

How achieved:

6. At the Final Judgment, regardless of whatever deeds or attributes he has to his favor, his skill as a writer will undoubtedly be found wanting.

Style:

How achieved:

7. A bad, bad writer is he.

Style:

How achieved:

8. As far as good writers are concerned, he isn't.

Style:

How achieved:

9. Such a writer is he as cannot frame an original idea nor conceive of the language to articulate it.

Style:

How achieved:

10. Were it possible to improve his skill, some few comments of constructive criticism might be a kindness. As it is, a complete and total silence on the subject of his writing ability is the epitome of benevolence.

Style:

How achieved:

Exercise 2: Experimenting with a Variety of Styles of Your Own Writing

Write each of the following sentiments in as many different styles as you can. After each, describe the style and explain how you achieved it (which words create which effect, etc.).

1. Education is important to future happiness.

   A.

   Style:

   How achieved:

   B.

   Style:

   How achieved:

   C.

   Style:

   How achieved:

   D.

   Style:

   How achieved:

E.

Style:

How achieved:

2. The pursuit of wealth is the source of all evil.

   A.

   Style:

   How achieved:

   B.

   Style:

   How achieved:

   C.

   Style:

   How achieved:

   D.

   Style:

   How achieved:

   E.

   Style:

   How achieved:

3. He is an effective representative of the people who elected him.

A.

Style:

How achieved:

B.

Style:

How achieved:

C.

Style:

How achieved:

D.

Style:

How achieved:

E.

Style:

How achieved:

4. _____ is the best of all holidays.

A.

Style:

How achieved:

B.

Style:

How achieved:

C.

Style:

How achieved:

D.

Style:

How achieved:

E.

Style:

How achieved:

5. Travel is the best way to broaden your perspective.

A.

Style:

How achieved:

B.

Style:

How achieved:

C.

Style:

How achieved:

D.

Style:

How achieved:

E.

Style:

How achieved:

Exercise 3: Changing Style

Choose a paragraph from an essay you have already written and rewrite it in at least two different styles. For each, describe the style and explain how you achieved it.

Exercise 4: Examining the Impact of Style on Readability

The following paragraph is written in a very formal, academic style. It has a Flesch Reading Ease score of approximately 35.5, which classifies it as a "difficult" passage. The 100-word sample on which this measure is based is marked by slashes.

Read the instructions that follow and note the effect each change has on the overall style of the piece.

/ Contrary to a common twenty-first-century misconception, science does not determine the nature of the Universe; it merely endeavors to offer a reasonable description of it. One of the primary goals of science has always been to describe reality without reliance on intuition, mere speculation, or an instinctive "understanding" of issues like the processes of life on earth, the movement of planets and other bodies in space, the very creation of the Universe. Prior to the nineteenth century, science's understanding of reality was, by and large, determined by observation and guess. If the guess made sense, it was accepted as / scientific theory. If what the physicist or biologist or chemist hypothesized did not conform to the conventional wisdom of the time, the scientist was labeled "heretic" and the hypothesis dismissed. During the 20th century, however, Science gained respectability and actually introduced several concepts that, even with significant explanation and numerous models, were simply irreconcilable with the common *perception* of reality. The consequence of the layperson's inability to resolve the discrepancy between the tenets of his or her personal faith— augmented by reason and personal logic—and the rapidly expanding sphere of scientific inquiry is a polarized society not unlike that of medieval Europe.

Instructions:

Each of the sentences from the above paragraph has been reprinted in the following exercise. Complete the following steps for each:

A. Count the words in each sentence.

B. Indicate which is the longest sentence and which is the shortest.

C. Label each sentence according to type (simple, compound, complex, etc.).

D. Identify any sentence elements that might increase the difficulty of the sentence (e.g., inverted word order, uncommon punctuation, interruptive phrases and/or clauses).

E. List three or four difficult words (three or more syllables) and suggest an easier replacement for each.

F. Rewrite each sentence to simplify it:

- where possible, break single compound, complex, and compound-complex sentences into several simpler sentences

- remove any sentence elements you identified as challenging

- substitute the difficult words you identified with your simpler suggestions

- be careful to maintain the academic tone of the sentence while simplifying the style.

1. Contrary to a common twenty-first-century misconception, science does not determine the nature of the Universe; it merely endeavors to offer a reasonable description of it.

Number of words: *25*   **Is this the longest or shortest sentence?:** *No*

Type of sentence: *compound*

Challenging sentence elements: *introductory phrase. Semi-colon instead of coordinating conjunction*

Difficult words: *misconception, determine, endeavors, merely*

Suggested replacements: *mistaken belief, create, tries, simply*

Revised sentence(s): *Many people mistakenly believe that science creates the nature of the Universe. The truth is, however, that science simply tries to describe it.*

Number of words per revised sentence: *12, 11*

Type(s) of sentence(s): *complex, complex*

2. One of the primary goals of science has always been to describe reality without reliance on intuition, mere speculation, or an instinctive "understanding" of issues like the processes of life on earth, the movement of planets and other bodies in space, the very creation of the Universe.

Number of words: **Is this the longest or shortest sentence?:**

Type of sentence:

Challenging sentence elements:

Difficult words:

Suggested replacements:

Revised sentence(s):

Number of words per revised sentence:

Type(s) of sentence(s):

3. Prior to the nineteenth century, science's understanding of reality was, by and large, determined by observation and guess.

Number of words: **Is this the longest or shortest sentence?:**

Type of sentence:

Challenging sentence elements:

Difficult words:

Suggested replacements:

Revised sentence(s):

Number of words per revised sentence:

Type(s) of sentence(s):

4. If the guess made sense, it was accepted as scientific theory.

Number of words: **Is this the longest or shortest sentence?:**

Type of sentence:

Challenging sentence elements:

Difficult words:

Suggested replacements:

Revised sentence(s):

Number of words per revised sentence:

Type(s) of sentence(s):

5. If what the physicist or biologist or chemist hypothesized did not conform to the conventional wisdom of the time, the scientist was labeled "heretic" and the hypothesis dismissed.

    Number of words: **Is this the longest or shortest sentence?:**

    Type of sentence:

    Challenging sentence elements:

    Difficult words:

    Suggested replacements:

    Revised sentence(s):

    Number of words per revised sentence:

    Type(s) of sentence(s):

6. During the 20th century, however, Science gained respectability and actually introduced several concepts that, even with significant explanation and numerous models, were simply irreconcilable with the common *perception* of reality.

    Number of words: **Is this the longest or shortest sentence?:**

    Type of sentence:

    Challenging sentence elements:

    Difficult words:

    Suggested replacements:

    Revised sentence(s):

    Number of words per revised sentence:

    Type(s) of sentence(s):

7. The consequence of the layperson's inability to resolve the discrepancy between the tenets of his or her personal faith—augmented by reason and personal logic—and the rapidly expanding sphere of scientific inquiry is a polarized society not unlike that of medieval Europe.

Number of words: **Is this the longest or shortest sentence?:**

Type of sentence:

Challenging sentence elements:

Difficult words:

Suggested replacements:

Revised sentence(s):

Number of words per revised sentence:

Type(s) of sentence(s):

8. Rewrite the paragraph using your revised sentences and then complete the instructions that follow.

   a. Separate the first 100 words from the rest of the paragraph with slashes (/).

   b. Count the number of sentences in this 100-word sample (count a partial sentence as .5).
      Divide 100 by the number of sentences.
      100/Number of sentences = _____ (Average Sentence Length)

   c. Count the number of **syllables** in this 100-word sample.
      Divide the number of syllables by 100.
      Number of syllables/100 = _____ (Average Syllables per Word)

d. Calculate the following:

206.835 − (1.015 x Average Sentence Length) − (84.6 x Average Syllables per Word) = Flesch Reading Ease measurement

On this scale, the higher the score (maximum of 100), the easier the passage is to read.

e. The original passage had a score of 35.5. Have you increased or decreased the readability of the passage (i.e., made the passage easier or more difficult to read)?_____

f. What would you need to do if you wanted to further increase the readability (make it easier to read)?

g. What would you need to do if you wanted to make the passage more challenging?

Exercise 5: Experimenting with Style and Readability

Select an essay you have already written and perform the following steps to determine the paper's readability level.

1. *Select a representative or typical 100-word sample.*

2. *Count the number of sentences in your 100-word sample (count a partial sentence as .5).*

3. *Divide 100 by the number of sentences.*

4. *100/Number of sentences = _____ (Average Sentence Length)*

5. *Count the number of syllables in your100-word sample.*

6. *Divide the number of syllables by 100.*

7. *Number of syllables/100 = _____ (Average Syllables per Word)*

8. *Calculate the following:*
   206.835 – (1.015 x Average Sentence Length) – (84.6 x Average Syllables per Word) = Flesch Reading Ease measurement

   On this scale, the higher the "score" (maximum of 100), the easier the passage is to read.

9. *Now examine your sample **sentence by sentence** as you did in Exercise 2:*

   Number of words: **Is this the longest or shortest sentence?:**

   Type of sentence:

   Challenging sentence elements:

   Difficult words:

   Suggested replacements:

Revised sentence(s):

Number of words per revised sentence:

Type(s) of sentence(s):

10. *If your essay's original readability score was **under 50**, revise each sentence to increase its readability.*
*If your essay's original readability score was **over 50**, revise each sentence to make the essay more challenging.*

Revised sentence(s):

Number of words per revised sentence:

Type(s) of sentence(s):

11. *Now rewrite your essay and perform another readability study. Have you succeeded in increasing or decreasing its readability?*

Writing Opportunity: *The Research Paper/Extended Essay: Using Research to Argue a Point*

Many academic courses and programs require a major research paper or essay as an exit requirement—something you must do to demonstrate that you are qualified to receive your diploma, degree, or certification. This research project includes three purposes:

1. to demonstrate the depth of your knowledge and understanding of a particular aspect of the course material

2. to demonstrate your ability to learn something independently and report back intelligently what you have learned and how you learned it

3. to demonstrate your ability to plan, execute, and complete a major project with minimal (or no) assistance or coaching by a teacher.

The extended research project allows you to demonstrate knowledge, the ability to learn independently, and the ability to communicate what you have learned intelligently with other knowledgeable persons.

Step 1: *Choose your topic*

This is one of the most important steps of the entire project. You must consider the breadth vs. depth issue. As you have already learned, and as writing instructor and editor William Zinsser has already commented in the previous books, you want more depth. You want to study a small part of the topic as deeply as you can.

To help you arrive at a sufficiently narrow topic, it might be helpful to think in terms of a research question.

Examples:

> **Topic:** *Jay Gatsby and Willie Loman as Tragic Heroes*
>
> **Research Question:** *To what extent do Jay Gatsby in F. Scott Fitzgerald's The Great Gatsby and Willie Loman in Arthur Miller's The Death of a Salesman meet the established Aristotelian and Shakespearean criteria for the tragic hero?*

> **Topic:** *The Romantic Hero as Precursor for the Twentieth-Century Anti-Hero*
>
> **Research Question:** *How do the isolation and antagonism toward social norms of Mary Shelley's Victor Frankenstein and Lord Byron's Manfred indicate a shift in the notion of who and what is "heroic"?*

> **Topic:** *Shakespeare's Use of the Supernatural*
>
> **Research Question:** *What dramatic and thematic roles do the witches in Shakespeare's Macbeth and the ghost in Hamlet play?*

Step 2: *Perform preliminary research*

Do a quick search to make certain that information on your topic exists and is accessible to you. This quick search needs to include:

- an Internet search (don't just rely on the popular search engines like Google and Yahoo. Learn to use more academic engines and metasearch engines like Search.com)

- a quick survey of books and magazine articles[1] available to you in your school's library

- a quick survey of books and magazine articles available to you in your local library

- a quick survey of books and magazine articles available to you in the libraries of any local colleges or universities.

In addition to finding that enough sources exist for your project, you might want to glance at some of the material offered by these sources. Not all articles on your subject will be helpful to you. If all of your sources in this preliminary step seem to point in a particular direction, you can take that into consideration when you draft your thesis.

Step 3: *Brainstorm and write your "shopping list."*

Focus on your research question. What specific information do you need to offer a complete and thoughtful answer? What background information will you have to provide?

Having done your preliminary search, you have an idea of what information you will be able to locate. Clearly, your "shopping list" should focus on what you know exists and you can find, not just on what you would present if you could find it.

---

[1]Just as in the research project in the previous book, your teacher will assume that you will actually use print as well as electronic sources.

Try to anticipate your reader's questions, his or her doubts, and the points he or she will find most difficult to grasp.

Time Clue: These steps really lay the foundation for your paper, so you do not want to rush them. You will probably need time to visit the different libraries you have access to (unless you're lucky and they all share a common database). You should give yourself several days to a week or two for this step.

Step 4: *Draft your initial thesis*

In a single sentence, state the governing idea of your paper. Let the thesis be, in essence, a one-sentence answer to your research question.

Examples:

Topic: *Jay Gatsby and Willie Loman as Tragic Heroes*

Research Question: *To what extent do Jay Gatsby in F. Scott Fitzgerald's The Great Gatsby and Willie Loman in Arthur Miller's The Death of a Salesman meet the established Aristotelian and Shakespearean criteria for the tragic hero?*

Thesis: *Although neither is born a deity or of high social rank, the established characters of Jay Gatsby in F. Scott Fitzgerald's The Great Gatsby and Willie Loman in Arthur Miller's The Death of a Salesman, the actions they perform, and the ends to which they fall, allow them both to be discussed in terms of the Aristotelian and Shakespearean models of the tragic hero.*

Topic: *The Romantic Hero as Precursor for the Twentieth-Century Anti-Hero*

Research Question: *How do the isolation and antagonism toward social norms of Mary Shelley's Victor Frankenstein and Lord Byron's Manfred indicate a shift in the notion of who and what is "heroic"?*

Thesis: *Twentieth-century readers and audience members may have considered the post-World War I anti-hero to have been a recent literary development, but this character's tendency to keep to himself and operate more or less outside the boundaries of social acceptability are foreshadowed in the Romantic Hero of the early nineteenth century, especially Mary Shelley's Victor Frankenstein and Lord Byron's Manfred.*

Topic: *Shakespeare's Use of the Supernatural*

Research Question: *What dramatic and thematic roles do the witches in Shakespeare's* Macbeth *and the ghost in* Hamlet *play?*

Thesis: *In his two best-known tragedies,* Macbeth *and* Hamlet, *Shakespeare uses the supernatural to set an eerie and suspenseful tone and introduce the question: To what extent is a human being the master of his or her own destiny?*

Note: Because your discussion of your thesis will require research, you cannot simply assume that you will find all of the information you will need to address it. Therefore, although you must have a sense of what your point is going to be, you must also be open to the possibility of having to revise this initial thesis.

Time Clue: This is a short step, as you already know something about your issue and already have an opinion. It should take less than an hour.

Remember: Do *not* state your thesis in the first person.

Step 5: *Write the title of your paper*

Again, the title is another means of focusing your thinking and your search for information. It might be enough simply to repeat your topic or rephrase your research question as a statement. Remember, however, that your title is the first clue to your reader whether he or she needs to read your full paper.

Examples:

Topic: *Jay Gatsby and Willie Loman as Tragic Heroes*

Research Question: *To what extent do Jay Gatsby in F. Scott Fitzgerald's The Great Gatsby and Willie Loman in Arthur Miller's The Death of a Salesman meet the established Aristotelian and Shakespearean criteria for the tragic hero?*

Thesis: *Although neither is born a deity or of high social rank, the established characters of Jay Gatsby in F. Scott Fitzgerald's The Great Gatsby and Willie Loman in Arthur Miller's The Death of a Salesman, the actions they perform, and the ends to which they fall, allow them both to be discussed in terms of the Aristotelian and Shakespearean models of the tragic hero.*

Title: *Modern Tragic Heroes: Jay Gatsby and Willie Loman*

Topic: *The Romantic Hero as Precursor for the Twentieth-Century Anti-Hero*

Research Question: *How do the isolation and antagonism toward social norms of Mary Shelley's Victor Frankenstein and Lord Byron's Manfred indicate a shift in the notion of who and what is "heroic"?*

Thesis: *Twentieth-century readers and audience members may have considered the post-World War I anti-hero to have been a recent literary development, but this character's tendency to keep to himself and operate more or less outside the boundaries of social acceptability are foreshadowed in the Romantic Hero of the early nineteenth century, especially Mary Shelley's Victor Frankenstein and Lord Byron's Manfred.*

Title: *The Romantic Hero as Precursor for the Twentieth-Century Anti-Hero*

Topic: *Shakespeare's Use of the Supernatural*

Research Question: *What dramatic and thematic roles do the witches in Shakespeare's Macbeth and the ghost in Hamlet play?*

Thesis: *In his two best-known tragedies, Macbeth and Hamlet, Shakespeare uses the supernatural to set an eerie and suspenseful tone and to introduce the question: to what extent is a human being the master of his or her own destiny?*

Title: *Dramatic and Thematic Roles of the Supernatural in Shakespeare's Macbeth and Hamlet*

Step 6: *Write your (first) outline*

As you organize your ideas to draft your outline, you will have to take several important factors into consideration:

- How much about your topic does your reader already know?

- How much background information will you have to give before beginning your actual discussion?

- Given your research question and thesis, what areas of development are inevitable? What should be avoided?

- Given your knowledge of your reader, what must you establish first (sub-point A) before moving on to sub-points B and C?

It is always a good idea to try out multiple versions of your outline.

> **Time Clue:** Give yourself several days. Always keep in mind your thesis, your research question, and knowledge of the sources you are going to be able to find.

Step 7: *Look at your sources and take notes*

> **Remember** that, when you were writing an essay of a few paragraphs, it was relatively easy to rush through the outline stage and simply rewrite an essay that didn't work, moving around paragraphs, etc. This project, however, will probably be comparatively long. The larger the project, the more information you will need, and the more difficult it will be to track, arrange, and rearrange that information. If you put real thought into your outlines, you would save yourself a lot of frustration as your final deadline approaches.

Stick to the information you said you needed in your shopping list and your outline. Do not allow a wealth of fascinating—but irrelevant—information to distract you from answering your research question.

Step 8: *(Re-)Organize your ideas (the revised outline)*

By now, you should have a much better handle on the information you're going to present. Before you write your first draft, make certain your outline reflects the best means of building your case for your reader.

Time Clue: Steps 7 and 8 are actually the bulk of the assignment. You should take one or more months, depending on how long you have to complete this project.

Step 9: *Write your first draft*

As always, make it as good as you can. You already have your information and a clear, well-thought-out organizational plan. Composing your first draft should take only as much time as it takes your hands to write or keyboard it physically.

When you quote or present information from a source that is not common knowledge, cite it with an MLA in-text citation and include the source in a list of works cited at the end of the paper. (See Appendix 2)

Time Clue: One or two days, depending on the length of the paper and the amount of time you've been given to complete it.

Step 10: *Write your abstract*

Just as you did in Trait 5, you need to write a brief synopsis of your paper as a means of making certain you have addressed the points raised in your research question and thesis. If the abstract of the paper written does not answer the research question, use it to find where you stray from your thesis and fix it when you revise.

Step 11: *Revise and rewrite your draft*

Set your draft aside for at least a day so that you can look at it with fresh eyes. Read your draft and consider:

- Is your thesis clear?

- Have you offered enough (but not too much) background information?

- Do you have enough information to clarify the issue to someone with limited knowledge on your subject? Does your information convince a reader that your thesis is valid?

- Is all of the information you present relevant to your thesis? Have you answered your research question?

- Is your evidence factual and objective, or do you rely on emotional appeals and sentimentalism?

- Have you gathered your evidence from credible sources, and have you made their credibility clear to your reader?

- Is your information presented in a logical order so that you are leading your reader to accept your conclusion as reasonable and valid?

If you have time, give your revised draft to one or more other people to read and critique. *This is another important step. Even professional writers have friends or writing groups with whom they share their work before it is finished and ready to be submitted for publication.*

Time Clue: Depending on the length of the paper, you will probably want two or three days for this step. Remember that the longer your paper is, the longer it will take to read, and the longer it will take to revise—especially if you find you need any kind of substantial rewriting.

Finally, create a new, clean draft of the paper.

Step 12: *Revise your abstract*

If you are required to submit your abstract with the project, revise your abstract to reflect whatever changes you made in the paper.

Step 13: *Turn in your paper.*

Appendix One:

Scoring Guide for the Proficient Level

DEVELOPMENT OF IDEAS

14 = ACCOMPLISHED
There are enough details, examples, anecdotes, supporting facts, etc. to give the reader a strong discussion. There is no needless information. Every word, phrase, clause, and sentence contributes to the main idea.

13 = The discussion is complete and sharply focused.

12 = The discussion is complete and focused.

11 = The discussion is complete and focused, but the reader is left with a sense that the topic has not really been exhausted.

10 = PROFICIENT
The main idea of the essay is clear. There is almost enough information for a full and complete discussion, but the reader is left with a few unanswered questions. The focus of the essay is clear, with a few lapses.

ORGANIZATION

14 = ACCOMPLISHED
The organizational plan of the essay seems inevitable given the topic, purpose, and audience.

13 = The essay flows so that the reader gets a sense of where the discussion is leading and understands how it has been put together.

12 = The structure of the essay helps the reader understand the information and follow the point.

11 = The organizational plan is clear, original, and logical. It does not detract from the reader's appreciation of the discussion, but does not enhance it either.

10 = PROFICIENT
The organizational plan of the essay is clear and original, and appropriate; but is not necessarily the best plan for the subject, purpose, and audience.

SENTENCE STRUCTURE AND VARIETY

14 = **ACCOMPLISHED**

The writer's sentence formation choices reflect a thorough understanding of the topic and how best to communicate it to meet the needs of the audience and the purpose of the writing.

13 = Variety in sentence structure and length generally contributes to the overall impact of the essay, but opportunities to communicate more clearly or to enliven the essay with sentence variety are sometimes missed.

12 = Variety in sentence structure and length enhances the overall clarity and impact of the essay.

11 = Variety in sentence structure and length is used to strengthen the impact of the essay.

10 = **PROFICIENT**

Sentence formation is adequate to meet the needs of the subject, audience, and purpose.

CONVENTIONS OF WRITTEN ENGLISH

14 = ACCOMPLISHED
Language is skillfully used throughout the essay. Sentence structure, punctuation, and artful use of Poetic License contribute significantly to the overall impact of the piece.

13 = Errors resulting from experimentation with form and usage are infrequent and do not interfere with the reader's understanding.

12 = Errors resulting from experimentation with form and usage do not severely interfere with the reader's understanding, but suggest the need for editing and minor revision.

11 = Having gained control over conventions, the writer begins to experiment with new constructions, usages, etc., for effect of communication. This experimentation, however, may result in awkward, incorrect, or inappropriate usage that requires careful editing and some revision to correct.

10 = PROFICIENT
The essay is free of surface errors (grammar, spelling, punctuation, etc.).

WORD CHOICE

14 = ACCOMPLISHED
Word choice, including use of figurative devices, reflects a thorough understanding of the topic and how best to communicate it in order to meet the needs of the audience and the purpose of the writing.

13 = Words are vivid and concrete without sounding forced or overworked. Figurative devices are appropriate and unaffected, adding clarity, meaning and interest to the essay.

12 = Word choice is specific, clear, and vital. Powerful nouns and verbs replace weaker words and phrases. Similes, metaphors, allusions are appropriate and add clarity, meaning and interest to the essay. Word choice and use of figurative language is fluent and effective.

11 = Word choice is specific, clear, and appropriate to the audience, topic, and purpose. Specific words replace vague, general terms. Similes, metaphors, allusions, etc.—while at times strained or not fully appropriate—add meaning and interest to the essay.

10 = PROFICIENT
Word choice shows evidence of awareness of the needs of the audience and the demands of the topic and purpose. Figurative devices are, for the most part, original and appropriate.

VOICE

14 = ACCOMPLISHED

The narrative voice of the essay is a natural and integral part of the piece, establishing the author's attitude toward the subject and the audience as well as communicating the ideas and information of the essay in a way that invites the reader to continue reading.

13 = Narrative voice is a natural result of the writer's language choices and is appropriate for the topic, purpose, and audience.

12 = The narrative voice of the essay seems inevitable, given the topic, purpose, and audience. Language is precise and fully controlled.

11 = The narrative voice of the essay is consistent and appropriate for the topic, purpose, and audience. Language is precise and fully controlled.

10 = PROFICIENT

Narrative voice is appropriate to the topic, purpose, and audience are clear and balanced, but largely overstated or forced—voice for the sake of voice.

Appendix Two:

Recap of MLA Documentation

1. **What is documentation?**
   Documentation is giving credit where credit is due: acknowledging the sources from which you got information for your paper or essay.

2. **Why must I be so careful about documenting my sources?**
   To present someone else's words as if they were your words, or to present information you got from someone else without giving that person credit is unfair, unethical, and illegal.

   Remember that intellectual property is just as real as physical property. To commit either plagiarism or copyright infringement is to steal someone else's property and is punishable by law.

3. **What are the absolute basics of proper documentation?**
   The Works Cited Page that lists every source of information you used in creating the essay, paper, report, or whatever. In your English classes, foreign language classes, and most other humanities classes, you will use the format prescribed by the Modern Language Association (MLA).

   The in-text citation that states where you got a particular bit of information or whose words you are quoting.

4. **Under what circumstances must I include a Works Cited Page in my essay or paper?**
   Every time you consult a source that is outside of your own body of knowledge, you should include a Works Cited Page at the end of your paper.

5. **What information must I include in the Works Cited Page?**
   A works cited entry for a book would look like this:

   Last, First. <u>Title of Book</u>. City: Publishing Company, copyright.

   Pearl, Matthew. <u>The Poe Shadow</u>. New York: Random House, 2006.

   A works cited entry for a magazine or newspaper article would look like this:

Last, First. "Title of Article" <u>Name of Newspaper or Magazine</u> date of issue (European style): page number.

Conchina, Laura M. "Matthew Pearl's Sophomore Novel Triumphs" <u>Literary Weekly Review</u> 22 June 2006: 32.

Dunnel, Barbara. "Another Pearl of Great Price." <u>New York Herald Journal</u> 23 May 2006, natl.ed.: C8.

A works cited entry for a web site would look like this:

<u>Title of Article or Web Site</u>. Author or producer of web information, copyright. Universal Resource Locator (URL).

<u>Author Spotlight: Matthew Pearl</u>. Random House, Inc., 2006. <http://www.randomhouse.com/author/results.pperl?authorid=23463>

Remember that every detail of the above format is important to replicate in your documentation.

Also, remember that the *MLA Handbook* recommends underlining material that is italicized in print.

Finally, don't spend your time trying to memorize the format for each type of entry; instead, find a good style sheet or handbook that provides examples of each type of source and learn how to follow it.

6. **Under what circumstances must I include an in-text citation in my essay or paper?**
   - Direct quotations.
   - Close paraphrases.
   - Summaries.

7. **Why must I use in-text citations for these uses?**
   a. It's all about authority and credibility
   b. You are not (yet) an expert in your own right
   c. You have the right to your opinion, but it needs to be an *informed* opinion
   d. If you do not cite your sources, your paper is no better than one written by a student who did no research at all.

8. **Doesn't that mean that *everything* in my paper will be cited and documented?**
    It does not. In fact, if you find yourself citing and documenting every sentence, every paragraph, every bit of information and insight you present, *you* have not contributed enough to the discussion. What you are writing is an elementary-level report, not a thesis-based research paper.

9. **What information must I include in the in-text citation?**
    a. In-text citations from the sources you have listed on the Works Cited Page above would look like this:

    (Pearl 87)

    (Conchina 34)

    (Dunnel C12)

    If there is no stated author, then an abbreviated form of the title will be sufficient.

    (Author Spotlight: Matthew Pearl)

    These are the forms for citing *all* information from your sources, whether it be in the form of a direct quotation, paraphrase, or summary.

    Important Variation: If you attribute a quotation or paraphrase to the source in the body of your paper, then you omit the author's name from the material in the parentheses.

    For example:
    (No attribution in the text):
    Some scientists still cling to the theory that the moon is made of green cheese: "Clearly, the quality of light the full moon casts on the landscape is consistent with sunlight reflecting off a huge cheese ball" (Stilton 293).

    (Attribution in the text—direct quotation):
    Some scientists still cling to the theory that the moon is made of green cheese. As Brie Stilton notes, "Clearly, the quality of light the full moon casts on the landscape is consistent with sunlight reflecting off a huge cheese ball" (293).

    (Attribution in the text—paraphrase):
    Some scientists still cling to the theory that the moon is made of green

cheese. Brie Stilton suggests that the light of the full moon is the type that would be created by sunlight reflecting off a ball of cheese (293).

When you have attributed the quotation to the source in the body of your paragraph, you do not need to repeat the author's name in the parenthetic citation.

Notice how the word "that" introduces a paraphrase, *not* a direct quotation.

Correct: Jane said, "I want to go home."
Correct: Jane said that she wanted to go home.
Incorrect: Jane said that, "I want to go home."

b. If you have more than one source by the same author on your Works Cited Page, follow the same logic about attribution and author's name and add an abbreviated version of the title of the specific source you are citing.

For example:
(No attribution in the text):
Some scientists still cling to the theory that the moon is made of green cheese: "Clearly the quality of light the full moon casts on the landscape is consistent with sunlight reflecting off a huge cheese ball" (Stilton, When it Sits on a Ritz 293).

(Attribution in the text—direct quotation):
Some scientists still cling to the theory that the moon is made of green cheese. As Brie Stilton notes, "Clearly the quality of light the full moon casts on the landscape is consistent with sunlight reflecting off a huge cheese ball" (When it Sits on a Ritz 293).

(Attribution in the text—paraphrase):
Some scientists still cling to the theory that the moon is made of green cheese. Brie Stilton suggests that the light of the full moon is the type that could be created by sunlight reflecting off a ball of cheese (When it Sits on a Ritz 293).

Important Variation: If you choose to mention the title of the source in the body of the paragraph, then you do not need to repeat that information in the parentheses.

For example: Some scientists still cling to the theory that the moon is made of green cheese. In her memoir, When it Sits on a Ritz, astrolonomer-psychic

Brie Stilton suggests that the light of the full moon is the type that could be created by sunlight reflecting off a ball of cheese (293).

Note the logic. Attribution, citation, and documentation formats are based on the principles of giving your reader all of the information he or she might need to locate the source and verify the accuracy of the information, while at the same time saving you from having to repeat author, title, and other publication data.

Note 1: Don't try to memorize all of the forms and variations; get a good style sheet or handbook and learn how to follow the models.

Note 2: Note that there is no punctuation between the author's name and the page number, nor is the page number indicated by any abbreviation (pg., p., pp., etc.).

c.   If you find yourself citing the same source two or more times consecutively, the first time, you need to use the full citation. Each consecutive time after that, you need only supply the page number (or section and page number, if appropriate).

If you cite a *different* source and then return to the first, you must return to the full citation, which includes both author and page number. Remember, your goal is to be absolutely clear to your reader where you have gotten the information you are presenting, while also sparing him or her from unnecessary repetition.

d.   If you find that you have listed all of the pertinent citation information in the text of your paper, you will have *no* parenthetical citation.

The simile in lines 22 and 23 of Act IV, scene ii, of *Macbeth* clearly foreshadows...

Note that *none* of these variations changes your need to list all of the pertinent information in the proper format on your works cited page.